Winning Your Husband Back

Before It's Too Late

Gary Smalley

Dr. Greg Smalley

THOMAS NELSON PUBLISHERS®

Nashville

Copyright © 1999 by Gary Smalley

All rights reserved. Written permission must be secured from the publisher to use or reproduce any part of this book, except for brief quotations in critical reviews or articles.

Published in Nashville, Tennessee, by Thomas Nelson, Inc.

Unless otherwise noted Scripture quotations are from the HOLY BIBLE: NEW INTERNATIONAL VERSION®. Copyright © 1973, 1978, 1984 by International Bible Society. Used by permission of Zondervan Publishing House. All rights reserved.

Scripture quotations noted KJV are from the KING JAMES VERSION of the Holy Bible.

Scripture quotations noted NASB are from the NEW AMERICAN STANDARD BIBLE®, Copyright © The Lockman Foundation 1960, 1962, 1963, 1968, 1971, 1972, 1973, 1975, 1977. Used by permission.

Scripture quotations noted NLT are from the *Holy Bible*, New Living Translation, Copyright © 1996. Used by permission of Tyndale House Publishers, Inc., Wheaton, Illinois 60189. All rights reserved.

Library of Congress Cataloging-in-Publication Data

Smalley, Gary.
   Winning your husband back / Gary Smalley, Greg Smalley.
      p.   cm.
   ISBN 0-7852-7044-2
      1. Wives—Religious life. 2. Marriage—Religious aspects—Christianity.
   I. Smalley, Greg. II. Title.
   BV4527.S57 1999
   248.8'435—dc21   99-26389
                                                                CIP

Printed in the United States of America
1 2 3 4 5 6 7 BVG 04 03 02 01 00 99

To Norma,
who for thirty-four years has been my best friend,
companion, lover, and encourager.
Thank you for winning me back.
—Gary

To the three people who remind me daily of what
matters most in marriage and in life:
Erin, Taylor, and Madalyn.
With all my love.
—Greg

Contents

Acknowledgments

This book represents the contributions of many people who struggle to better understand marriage and to help married couples. First and foremost, we acknowledge our friend, mentor, and colleague Dr. Gary Oliver, who has provided much wisdom and insight, both personally and professionally over the years. We would like to acknowledge Dr. Larry Keefauver for the diligent and professional work he provided during the development of this manuscript.

We also deeply appreciate the talents and support of Terry Brown and the staff at Smalley Relationship Center. Thank you, Jim and Suzette Brawner, Jimmy Funderburk, Roger Gibson, Sheila Green, Debbie Meyer, John Nettleton, Michael Smalley, Norma Smalley, Sheila Smethers, Lori Vanderpool, and Terri Woolsey.

We would like to express our deep sense of appreciation for the individuals and couples who have shared their lives and marital journeys with us. Thank you, Trish and Rick Tallon, Shelly Creed, Debbie-Jo White, Cary Jones, Kay

Acknowledgments

Hammer, Kim Feder, Melissa Tomlinson, Wendi Schroeder, and Susan Butterfield.

We thank Mike Hyatt for his enthusiasm in developing this project. We also thank Cindy Blades and the staff at Thomas Nelson for their support and expertise during this process.

Most important, we thank the Lord for His blessings and for making so many things plainly evident for our learning and growth.

Chapter . . . .
One . . . .

Develop an Overall Plan

The Life of a Driver

I was the latest and best new driver when a fairly new golfer bought me. Right away we were a special team. With me he hit the ball farther and straighter.

My golfer told everyone how special I was and how he had never played better because of me. He took me into the clubhouse after a round and continued to sing my praises. When we got home, he polished and shined me and took me into his room between uses instead of leaving me in the garage with his other clubs. I felt so special and pampered. I tried to help turn through the shot and climb high on the backswing and follow through.

Occasionally, we hit a ball into the water or the rough, but we won many tournaments and he won lots of money with me. Sometimes I could feel his grip tighten or we swung too fast and we mishit a ball. On those occasions, he would sometimes become very emotional and blame me, but then he cheered up, regained his balance, and we continued winning.

We began playing more and more and his grip steadily tightened and he swung harder. We hit balls in all sorts of bad places. My golfer became progressively more frustrated and angry and blamed me every time. He would throw me angrily into the bag without my cover. Once he even threw me into the lake only to come to get me later. I tried to follow his swing; but the line and tempo were off. I couldn't turn through the shot as before.

His anger grew and he quit taking me into the clubhouse after a round or into his room at night. He even told everyone that he didn't know why he had bought me and that he had never hit well with me. I was so insulted and hurt.

Several people suggested lessons with the "pro," but my golfer refused, saying that there was nothing wrong with his swing. He said the faults were the crowding of the course, the weather, his headache, the noise made by the other golfers, and the club—that I was too long, too stiff, too light, weighted incorrectly, and so on.

Finally, one day he exploded after a bad shot and threw me down on the ground after hitting the cart with me. He was so angry! When we got home, he threw me into the corner of the garage. Thank goodness I had my cover on.

I didn't go onto the course anymore. The new clubs he bought to replace me soon joined me in the corner of the garage, saying that his grip was too tight for them, also, and that he swung too fast.

One day, I was put back in his bag and taken to the golf

professional for lessons. A swing flaw was corrected here and there. Some of my dints were fixed and I was regripped and polished. Neither partner was changed, but rather, both were updated. Soon we were hitting the ball far and straight, just like before. We began winning again and were the envy of the other players.

This was an "emotional word picture"[1] we received, written by a woman whose husband had walked out of their marriage. She went on to write, "David, I want you to understand how I feel about our life together and divorce. Until you wanted out of the relationship and would not seek a life with me, I had always felt secure in the assurance that we were committed to each other for a lifetime. It was the cement foundation that gave me the awareness that whatever difficulties we faced, we would work to solve them together—that we were fully committed. I never doubted your commitment. Now I feel like the driver in the garage. It only takes the decision and the 'golf pro' to resurface the commitment with new skills and knowledge and build a deeper intimacy. It takes a decision."

As the above writer understood, the process of winning your husband back requires several important ingredients, like finding "golf pros" (Christ, experts, family, friends, mentors, and other support), making a decision to love and remain married, and developing new skills and knowledge. Our hope is that you will find the keys to these important issues, as well as others, within the pages of this book. Join us as we begin the journey of winning back your husband.

This Book Is for You!

This book is for women who have noticed a distance forming between them and their husband. That gap may be a Grand Canyon chasm that seems virtually impossible to span. Or it may be a crack that ever so slowly widens and uproots the foundations of your marriage like a tree root gradually pushing against a sidewalk until first a crack then a fissure breaks through. What was once a smooth, solid, and level walk together is now uneven and breaking apart.

The distance growing in your relationship may have been suddenly precipitated or slowly and imperceptibly prying apart and stretching the seams of closeness that once knit you together in a love you expected to last forever.

Winning Your Husband Back is a book for you if you're a wife . . .

- whose husband may be emotionally gone but not physically absent.
- who has been involved in an affair and now desires to restore your marriage.
- whose husband has been in an affair and you want to win him back.
- whose lifestyle or career has kept you too busy to stay emotionally or physically close to your husband.
- who has focused on relationships with your children and neglected your husband.

Determine Where You Are

It's time to assess where your marital relationship stands right now. How much distance is there between you and your husband? Put an *X* on the continuum below marking where the relationship is:

Beginning to Grow Apart	Emotional Separation	Physical Separation	Alienation	Divorce

The farther you are to the right of center, the more difficult it will be to reverse the direction you are headed. In making this assessment, you have taken an important step. You have faced the reality of where you are.

If you find it difficult to mark the continuum, you may still be in denial. Denial is the refusal to accept or to see circumstances as they really are. Tell yourself the truth. If you have a mentor, ask her where she would put an *X* on the line. See how close your perception of reality is to hers.

Once you have admitted where the relationship is, you have some choices to make.

1. You can decide to remain angry and blame yourself or your husband. This will result in being stuck where you are until the pain becomes so unbearable that you finally admit, "I can't go on like this forever." Anger and blame become terribly self-destructive as well as deadly to any possible future reconciliation with your husband.

Anger is to marriage what termites and rot are to trying to rebuild a home. Why put up new Sheetrock and wallpaper on a wall whose studs are eaten away by termites? While the surface may look great for the short-term, the building is doomed to collapse until both the termites and rot are removed.

The same is true for your marital relationship. Being stuck in the mire of anger and blame will only cause your marriage to deteriorate further until it finally disintegrates.

2. You can decide to grieve and stay depressed. When a patient is terminally ill, the family may start grieving over their loss even though the ill loved one is still breathing. Terminally ill patients often report that they feel abandoned by family who have already started preparing for death while the patient still lives. If you are grieving over your marriage, you may already be filling out its death certificate. What husband would want to be around a constantly depressed wife? If the marriage isn't dead, don't bury it prematurely.

3. You can decide to bargain with God or your husband. This attitude is characterized by, "If you do _____, then I will do _____." Bargaining seeks to manipulate God or a husband into being who we want them to be or into doing what we want them to do. If a wife decides to take this action, she tries to negotiate with her estranged husband the terms of their reconciliation. Or she tries to get God to accept and bless her plan for putting the marriage back together. Bargaining is doomed to dismal failure. It will only push your husband farther away.

4. Or, you can simply decide to assess the situation realistically, accept reality, and refuse to stay stuck. Now you are ready for the next step.

You have taken the first step, which is to recognize that distance exists between you and your husband—either physically or emotionally. He may or may not be living under the same roof as you. He may or may not want to work on rebuilding a marriage relationship. He is not the key; you are! If you desire to win him back, then it's time for you to start just as Norma did in our marriage years ago.

Too Close for Comfort—How Norma Won Me Back

Winning your husband back strikes close to home. I [Gary] know this subject well because it's almost too close for comfort; or should I say that my wife, Norma, knows well how to win her husband back—me! That's right. Early in our marriage, Norma and I faced the issue of how to come back together across the miles of relational distance that separated us. I have asked Norma to share with you in her own words how she began to lose me and how she took those first, crucial steps toward winning me back.

Six weeks after we were married in 1964, I started feeling very lonely. I had never felt that before as a single person, so I didn't really know what was happening. We were in a new city and lived in a new apartment. As I examined my feelings, trying to understand why I felt so alone and why I didn't feel super excited about being married, I realized that everything in Gary's life seemed more important than I was.

He was a full-time student and youth director at our new church. This meant long hours away from home studying and attending youth events such as basketball games. He was so swamped. Of course, by this time I was pregnant. That brought in another person who needed his time and attention. He tried to fit me in somewhere, but as the months passed by, we began to grow more and more distant from each other. I began to feel very lonely. We had never had relationship training. Therefore, I didn't know how to express my true feelings to get him to respond in a positive way. I would say in frustration, "You don't really spend any time with me. When you're not in school, you're over at the church counseling or meeting with young people. I don't know anyone at the church. I sit in church alone." I think he thought that I was being ridiculous. He would always answer defensively, "You knew when we got married that God would be first place in my life. That the people in ministry would be second, and you would be third." I think the saddest thing is that we did not have the insight to know that we should go for counseling.

Each time this negative interaction took place, the distance between us seemed to grow wider and wider. He usually walked away and I sat in silence, stuffing my feelings back further. The worst part was that I began to feel like a nag as I "reminded" Gary of my relational needs. It felt very hurtful. I think deeper than that I felt something was very wrong. But I didn't have the knowledge and training to figure it out. So I just accepted that and every so often would talk about it. Thus, this became our pattern for the first three years of our marriage.

There were many times I felt guilty for demanding to be a higher priority to my husband. I really respected his strong love for the Lord and his dedication to minister to people. Those were the very things that attracted me to him, the reason I really wanted to marry him. I couldn't figure out why I had this longing to be higher in his priorities. None of it really made sense to me. Most of the time I would hide my true feelings because I'd wear out during a confrontation. Gary has a much stronger personality and I like peace at all costs. So I would be silent, but hurting and longing inside.

During this time Gary had started going to a seminar put on by Bill Gothard. It was wonderful. It was the first light of hope that I saw at the end of this tunnel. Several times after the seminar, Gary asked me how I felt and earnestly wrote it down. But after several months, it had little effect. Now he was trying to become an expert in his field. That meant more time with the church people and with the youth group. He was in heaven professionally. The other thing that started to come into play was his personal time. On days off or during any free time, he wanted to watch football or go fishing with somebody. I grew more and more frustrated as I felt pushed a notch lower.

We began to argue more frequently, which only added more distance between us. So then he would say, "Hey, I have an opportunity to spend my day off fishing with some of the church men. What do you think?" I was insulted. Since his days and his evenings were spent at the church with these people, I couldn't believe that he would want to take off time from me and our small children to fish. It was one thing to submit to him doing God's work at the church. But I had to draw the line at fishing. Weren't we more important than a bass?

At the same time I remember the spiritual guilt trip I experienced for even saying how I felt, again feeling that a wife should always prefer what her husband wanted above her wants. But I still believed deep down inside that something was wrong. Something about his priorities seemed out of balance. But I didn't know how to confront him without feeling very mean inside. Rather than act that way in front of the children, I decided to let silence do my talking. This was how it was going to be and I would have to live with it.

About this time, Gary was getting more involved with Gothard's seminar in Chicago. The Lord started to work in his life and he became interested in what was wrong with me. If someone would have asked Gary, "Do you love your wife more than fishing?" He would have obviously said, "Absolutely." If they had asked him if he loved the youth or the church people more, he would have answered by this time, "No." But he didn't understand that he was not valuing me as one of his priorities.

One day Gary came home unexpectedly at lunchtime. The children were asleep. He asked me several questions that caused my anxiety to skyrocket. "Norma," he said gently, "what do you see as being wrong with our relationship? Why don't you feel that you're number one—an important priority in my life?" I stared at him in silence for a few seconds. I didn't want to answer. These times were so hard for me because they could last hours and might finally end with a "Proverbs 31 woman" lecture. But Gary was persistent. I rolled my eyes and thought to myself, *I'll do this one last time.*

We talked for hours—much like in the past; however, this time instead of receiving a reprimand to become more Proverbs 31–like, a light went on in Gary's head. He really understood what I was saying.

As Gary repeated things back to me I felt that he had the head knowledge, although I didn't have a lot of hope that there would be a change. But because of my lifelong commitment, there was no other choice. My faith in the Lord dictated that I accept that Gary did want to change. That he desired to learn about my needs. That was a real marking in time for us. He had been growing in his relationship with the Lord. He began to understand that I was fifth, even sixth place in his life. However, until I realized something about myself, I wasn't yet on the right path that would "win" my husband back.

Around this time, I began to realize that my level of relational satisfaction did not begin with my husband making me feel like a priority. Instead, I needed to reach out to him and begin to win him back in our marriage. This understanding was a foundational principle that I had to learn. Because of my commitment to our marriage I realized that I needed to become a team player. In other words, instead of my waiting for Gary to make changes, I needed to encourage him in what he was doing. I needed to praise him when he did little things, which seemed kind of ridiculous to me. They were so obvious, but I realized I had to let him know when he did something small that made me feel very important. When he said, "Tonight I don't want to go over to the church. I just want to be with you," I needed to make that a big thing so he could see some results. I would say to him, "Gary, you made me feel like such a priority when you stayed home instead of going to the church. Thank you." It was amazing. You could see his brain computing and analyzing my response: *If that's the response I get by staying home from church, imagine if I stayed home from fishing!* He began to make me truly feel like a priority that day. I learned a valuable lesson in those early years: You're more likely to get positive results when you build up someone for what they do right, than when you correct them for what they do wrong. Taking responsibility for myself became part of the foundation that God used to strengthen our marriage. I also had to be courageous at times when we slid backward. My responsibility was to share my feelings even when it meant a possible argument or worse—a lecture.

We were still not in a situation where we were getting any training in husband-wife relationships, other than what

Gary was getting from Bill Gothard, which really centered around his life with the Lord. Subsequently, my relationship with the Lord became a top priority. I was driven to start studying and started reading in Genesis to try to understand.

One of the neat things that I felt I received in Scripture was understanding that when a man and a woman marry, he is to leave his family and commit to her. It's God's perfect design. I didn't have to feel guilty that God wanted me to feel that I was number one. It wasn't selfish. Actually, when I felt like number six, it was like a thermometer that would inform Gary and let me know that we were not growing together—but in opposite directions. That was a tremendous boost for me to see that I need to be even more active in spending time talking with Gary about our relationship.

Now Is the Time to Start Winning Your Husband Back

I (Gary) am so proud of Norma. She didn't wait until I started doing things right before she began taking steps to draw closer to me. Notice that she took the initiative to begin to affirm and encourage me. Instead of nagging me about my overwork, she began to find ways to team up with me in those areas that were important to me. She also grew closer to God. And she stopped feeling guilty about wanting more from our relationship.

You may be on a slow slide or a rapid free fall toward separation or even divorce in your marriage. Either way, now is the best time for you to start winning your husband back through taking positive steps in loving the Lord, yourself, and your husband.

What's Your Plan?

Imagine building a home without a foundation or on a foundation of sand or mud. Renovating or redecorating your home would be senseless because at any moment the whole house could collapse because of the faulty foundation. The same is true of rebuilding a relationship with your husband. The original foundation for your marriage has disintegrated. Your house lies in shambles. Now that you have decided to start over, develop an overall plan to win your husband back.

When a certain room in your home is in disrepair or desperately needs renovating, simply moving the furniture around will not do. An interior designer would start at the foundation and work up, changing everything from flooring to wall coverings, window coverings, colors, furniture, and accessories. A complete overall plan or strategy would be necessary.

Likewise, winning your husband back necessitates more than simply rearranging the old stuff in your relationship. For example, you may decide to fight differently from the way you fought in the past, but if the same old furniture of unresolved anger is allowed to remain, then nothing will genuinely change in your marriage. Old mildewed carpet can ruin a room just like smelly, rotten anger from the past can ruin a marriage. As I said in *Making Love Last Forever*, the number one enemy of love in marriage is unresolved anger.

Let's return to our analogy of remodeling or building a house. You can begin to remodel a kitchen by taking a sledgehammer and beginning to knock out the cabinets or you can obtain drafted plans and hire a contractor to help you renovate step-by-step.

To renovate, we need paint, plaster, plumbing, electrical wiring, and much, much more. We may not want to gut the entire house. The antique fireplace may be a valuable keepsake while the old wool carpet must go. Whatever we incorporate into the new house, it will be done according to plan, not whim.

What You Will Discover in This Book

The same is true for winning your husband back. With a house, you need a master site plan or survey that shows how everything will be laid out on your land. In marriage, you need a plan that provides you with a vision for today and the next step for tomorrow. Furthermore, your plan must start at the foundation. What design sketches or blueprints can you make to reinforce or build a foundation?

Join us as we learn together how to bridge the gaps that can form in marriage through infidelity, insensitivity, anger, hurt, bad attitudes, and unloving words and actions. In this book you will learn the following key elements to winning your husband back:

1. Establish Christ as your fulfillment in life. Often we plug into the wrong sources of fulfillment: people, places, and things. The foundation of your home must be Christ.

2. Become whole. A house is only as clean and sound as the housekeeper is. Your home will be a reflection of you. How are you doing—in body, soul, and spirit?

3. Get support. As you take on the task of remodeling your home, it is vital to get assistance from other homeowners, builders, carpenters, painters, and professionals.

4. Discover ways to energize yourself during the remodeling process. The task of rebuilding your house from the ground up can be exhausting. We will describe four key elements that can provide instant energy to keep you going.

5. Honor your husband. There are many things around your house that are extremely valuable—like rare antiques. We will show you how to identify and honor your husband's antiques.

6. Open your husband's closed spirit. Over the years, you have knocked holes in the walls, spilled things on the carpet, ripped the curtains, and caused other kinds of damage around the house. We will show you how to reverse the damage you may have caused to your home.

7. Forgive your husband. Over the years, your husband has caused damage to your house as well. The remodeling process will not turn out with the beauty you envision unless you can first forgive the past damage.

8. Keep further damage from happening. Establishing new boundaries can help you to build protection around your house to protect it from further emotional and physical damage.

9. Communicate. Good communication that listens, starts softly, and responds positively can keep you close to your husband. Discover that when you are free to lose him, you are free to win him back.

10. Become a student of your husband. In order to successfully rebuild, renovate, renew, and restore your home, you must first learn what each room needs to be beautiful. We will help you to learn about your husband's most important relational needs.
11. What if he doesn't come back? Even if you are open to Christ and follow every principle within this book, your husband may choose not to respond to your rebuilding efforts. If this happens we will show you how to turn this into a victory.

Meet the Real "Experts"

In the following chapters, we will explore together how to win your husband back. We will be hearing from some wives who have shared their experiences with us about how they have sought to win their husbands back. What these women and scores of other couples have learned will help to encourage and strengthen your relationship not only with your husband but also with God and yourself.

Let us briefly introduce some of these wives to you now through a brief comment from each. You may find yourself feeling and saying the same types of things.

Debbie: It began with a distance that had been happening for years. We weren't communicating at all. Then I began to realize he was paying a lot of attention to the lady we were working with . . . he would spend a lot of time at dental appointments and came home late. He was seeing her. I finally said to him, "Well, it's me or her!"

Cindy: I was having a really tough time being emotionally supportive of him and he simply wasn't there for me. I had been sexually abused as a child. I needed his support but he had no clue how to treat a wife or how to be a husband. I looked to another man for support and got physically involved. I was anorexic, depressed, and suicidal. I was gone every weekend spending time with another man. I was angry with my husband, God, and myself. I needed him but didn't know how to respond to him.

Heidi: I had it all—a beautiful home, four wonderful children, and a prosperous lifestyle. Outwardly it looked to others like everything was right. Yet inside, I was dying. We had all the outward trappings of a relationship with each other and God, but inwardly there was nothing.

Sandi: The main reason I married my husband was because of his family devotion and loyalty. My family wasn't like that. I thought he would always be there for the kids and me. I always felt that in a husband's life his wife would come second to God. I never came second. I never came third. I never came fourth.

Brenda: I found that we were getting lost in busyness. It wasn't an affair thing. It was just busyness with work, other organizations, or overcommitting himself. I was getting lost in all the busyness. So what I started doing was to just let go of him. I pulled away and let him keep doing all his things.

Amber: When I got married, I took over and did what I wanted to do. Our home was not the way God intended our home to be. God at the head, man under Him, and then the wife. I knew the way we were doing it was wrong, because the burden was so heavy.

As these women will exemplify, your relationship with yourself is critically important in the quest to win your husband back. A good start to winning your husband back is to love yourself and love God. Centuries ago Jesus taught, "'You must love the Lord your God with all your heart, all your soul, and all your mind.' This is the first and greatest commandment. A second is equally important: 'Love your neighbor as yourself.'"[2] Before you can find the power to love your husband and perhaps win him back; you need to learn once again how to love God and yourself.

At the end of this journey you might have your husband back, or he might refuse to return. Either way, you will be living with the Lord and yourself for a lifetime. A winning relationship with God and self will sustain you regardless of how your marital relationship is resolved. Right now, if you are willing to work at loving yourself, God, and your husband with the hope of winning him back, then this book is for you.

Finally, you may ask, "Why should I take the initiative—the first step?" Someone has to—why not you? If you desire to win your husband back, then some risk is involved. Yes, hurt and rejection are possibilities. Taking a first step does not guarantee quick or easy success. It's hard, risky and, at times, painful. Nonetheless, beginning to reduce the distance between you and your husband through understanding him can bring a significant thaw to your cooling relationship. And regardless of your husband's reaction—positive or negative, you will have accepted and affirmed who you are and who he is in Christ. And that "win" can never be stolen from you regardless of how your husband chooses to respond to you!

Your house may be beginning to crumble or already be in complete shambles. Its condition does not determine its future. You do. Winning your husband back begins with your relationship with Christ! So let's get started!

Chapter . . . .
Two . . . .

Find Fulfillment in Life

Everyone longs to give themselves completely to someone. To have a deep soul relationship with another. To be loved thoroughly and exclusively. But to the Christian, God says:

> Wait, not until you are first satisfied, fulfilled, and content with being loved by Me can I bring you true love. You see, first you must give yourself totally and unreservedly to Me, discovering that only in Me is your satisfaction to be found. Only then, will you be capable of the perfect human relationship that I have for you.
>
> You will never be fully united with another until you are united with Me. Exclusive to anyone or anything else, I want you to stop planning, stop wishing and allow Me to bring it to you. You must keep watching and experiencing the satisfaction that I am, expecting Me to do the greatest of

things. Most importantly, keep listening and learning the things I show you. Just wait . . . That's all!

Don't be anxious, and don't worry. Don't look at the things others have received, or that I have given them. You just keep looking at Me, or you'll miss what I am teaching you. Then, when you're ready, I'll give you a love far more wonderful than any you will ever dream about.

Most of all, I want you to see in his flesh, a picture of your relationship with Me and enjoy the everlasting union of beauty, perfection, and love that I offer you. "Believe it and be satisfied."

My daughter, until you are ready—I am working even this moment to have you both ready at the same time. Until you are both satisfied and content with me and the life I have prepared for you; you won't be able to experience the love that exemplifies your relationship with Me, thus, perfect love.

The above, titled "Perfect Love," is a beautiful illustration of God's perfect design for our lives. He wants to become our "first love." From different painful experiences that I (Gary) have been through, I've learned that I was looking for love, peace, and joy in all the wrong places. In other words, I had spent a lifetime looking for a sense of significance and security. But I was looking in the wrong location. Since then, I've learned that we all have similar goals in life. If our lives were like a cup, each one of us would love to fill it with wisdom, love, joy, and peace. We'd like to have our lives overflow with positive emotions and genuine fulfillment. At a very early age, we begin to look for what we think can fill our cups with these positive qualities. Unfortunately, as I (Gary) wrote in *Joy That Lasts*, most of us look to one of three sources, or all three, for the fullness of life we really want. Yet, like a mirage, these sources shimmer with fulfillment but only bring dust to our souls.

Source #1—Looking to *people* to fill our cups. The first place many of us tend to look is to people. We think: *If I am to really have my needs met and be happy, I must have another person in my life.* However, those who look to people will ultimately find that they cannot fill their cup. Others can be frustrating and irritating and drain away as much emotional energy as they give—or more. Husbands can be a tremendous source of help and encouragement at times, but even they can disappoint us over the long haul. We can look to husbands as the source of positive emotions, but at times they, too, can punch holes in our emotional lives. Tragically, some people will have an affair to try to "fill their cup." The sweet taste of stolen waters may seem to fill one's life, but it's actually like drinking ice-cold salt water. The burning aftertaste of sin can burn huge holes in our cups and leave us emptier and more miserable than we ever imagined.

Source #2—Looking to *places* for fulfillment. "We need a home! That's it, we need a place with a beautiful view and trees that are the envy of the neighborhood. If only we had the right place to live in, our cup would be full." How many of us have echoed these words? Or perhaps, a vacation or a new office with a window—these certainly would fill our cup to the brim. Then we go to that remote island or buy that special home, live in it for a short while, and suddenly our life begins to go wrong. In part, that's true because the bigger the home, the more items to repair around the house. We can install a swimming pool in our yard, a fireplace in our living room, or buy a mountain cabin, but the yard, living room, or cabin won't keep us full. Why? In part because no matter how pretty or fulfilling places look, they don't fit inside our personal cups. Instead, they all have sharp edges that cut holes into our lives. What's more, the people we share them with are the people who drain our cups! But if people and places don't fill the deepest part of our lives, where do we turn to finally find love, peace, and joy?

Source #3—Looking to *things* for fulfillment. How about more money so we can buy more things? Many of us feel that if we just had more money, we'd be happier in life. But study after study of people who "strike it rich" shows this isn't the case. The more money we make, the more wisdom we must have to handle it. Now, I know many of us wouldn't mind learning that kind of wisdom. But to receive money, we normally have to pay a personal price. Thomas Carly once said, "For every person who can handle prosperity, there are a hundred who can't handle adversity." Money alone, and all the things it can bring, can't fill our lives with the kind of living water we desperately want. I've met people throughout the country who have little money and are miserable. And I've also met those with lots of money who are miserable. I've known people who have mountain cabins and third cars who feel fulfilled. And some people I know barely have bus fare, and they also feel fulfilled. Most people who depend on "things" to fill their cups end up looking for the one "perfect" job that will be the ticket to all their dreams. All jobs have work in common. And work doesn't always keep our cup full. It can drain us because of the people we work with, the place where we do our work, and the equipment we must use. Some of us try all our lives to acquire a key to a certain washroom in the company, or parking spaces with our names on them. When we receive them, however, what do we have? Are we finally being filled with wisdom, love, peace, and joy? Hardly. Just the opposite is often true.

Coming Up Empty in Life

At some times in our lives, we run headlong into an inescapable fact. Life is not fulfilling. It's actually often unfair and exhausting. We can never pour enough people, places, or things into our personal cups to keep our lives filled and overflowing with the contentment we want so much. No wonder so many people leading lives of emotional desperation consider suicide as a way out. By focusing on people, places, and things, we miss the positive emotions we want and are saddled with the very negative emotions we've tried all our lives to avoid! This is true of hurt feelings, worry, anxiety, fear, unrest, uncertainty, and confusion because we are depending on a person, place, or thing for "life."

We all face the temptation to look to people, places, and things to fill our cups. We're all selfish in wanting others to cooperate in meeting our needs right now. But those who are wise realize there is a pathway to freedom, away from that unfulfilled feeling.

Seeking First the Source of Life

As she wrote in her letter, Cindy realized the power of discovering the ultimate Source of life—Jesus Christ:

I was considering a divorce when I happened to see one of your infomercials with Frank and Kathie Lee Gifford. I figured, *What can it hurt?*, so I ordered the set of twelve videotapes, Hidden Keys to Loving Relationships. At the time, my husband and I had already been in marital counseling for three years. My husband, Scott, had given our marriage to the Lord, but I was not serving God in any capacity. In fact, I had been involved with another man for about five years. Scott willingly watched each tape with me, and made the decision to love and forgive me. Because of that, I would see small glimmers of hope for us as he attempted to implement your teachings. So, I never actually filed for divorce, but my heart was extremely cold toward him.

During those five years I was also dealing with flashbacks into my childhood, anorexia and bulimia, manic depression, and sexual abuse issues. My mind and life were a mess, to say the least. Somewhere in all of this a lightbulb went on. I realized that all of this "stuff" was just symptoms of a greater problem. I asked my psychiatrist to take me off all the medications. He told me, however, the side effects of stopping would be worse than any I was currently having. I thought, *How can it get worse?* I asked a few people from our church to pray and I never had a single side effect. Praise God!

As my mind cleared, I began to think that maybe there really is a God. Then my husband went to his first Promise Keepers stadium event. He came home a changed man. The ball really began to roll. Many times as we discussed marital issues, my husband would say, "Remember what Gary Smalley talked about in the tapes?" All this time God was working on me. Finally on April 30, 1996, God broke down the walls around my hardened heart. Although I couldn't stand to be in the same room as my husband, I was no longer having an affair. That night I cried out to the Lord, "Lord, change me!" Within forty-eight hours I began loving my husband in a new way. We began watching your videos again, trying together to put into practice what you teach. As God began to restore me and our marriage, I prayed that God would use us to touch others' lives. Now we are sharing these videos with a small group of couples in our church, and we have started our own accountability group. Over the past year I have experienced God's healing power in both my mental life and my physical life. It is nothing short of a miracle!

Matthew 6:33 clearly shows us our Source of life that Cindy wrote about. "But seek first his kingdom and his righteousness, and all these things will be given to you as well." In my life (Gary), when God is in first place, He promises to meet all my needs. I try to love God with all my heart. In other words, He's the highest priority in my life. When I focus on Jesus Christ as the sole Source of my life, an amazing thing happens. Because He loves me and actually possesses the wisdom, love, peace, and joy I've always wanted, He alone can overflow my cup. That's exactly what He promises to do for His children: "This love . . . surpasses knowledge—that you may be filled to the measure of all the fullness of God" (Eph. 3:19). Can you be any more filled than full? Absolutely not.

If I (Gary) ever start to feel worry, fear, hurt, or any other negative emotion, I thank God for it. Then I pray and ask forgiveness for focusing on something that is less than Himself. Finally, I ask Him alone to fill my life. Psalm 62 says that we are to wait and hope in God alone. He's our rock, our salvation, our rear guard, our hiding place. He's everything we'll ever need! Nothing on this earth compares to knowing Him (Phil. 3:7–9).

In chapter one, we introduced Heidi. We would like to share her story of how Christ restored her and her marriage as He became her fulfillment in life.

Heidi drove Johnny farther away by trying to compete with his mistress and his business. Being in a family business, Johnny was taught growing up that the business came first, then the children, and finally the wife. She complained to him, "If I danced on top of a table while you were thinking about a business deal, I could never get your attention."

As she tried to pull his attention away from the business and more to her, Heidi's husband refused to talk about her concerns. "We don't have a problem, you do," he would retort.

So as Heidi began to come between Johnny and his mistress—the business—he simply worked harder and harder. On the other hand, Heidi began to drown her hurts in antidepressants and Valium.

I (Gary) know personally about the night she decided to leave him because I was there. Heidi and Johnny lived in the same town as Norma and I. One night as I was writing my book *Love Is a Decision*, I decided to go out on an errand. Norma was out of town and I locked myself out of the house! Being close to Johnny and Heidi's home, I stopped by their house and they invited me to spend the night with them until I could get a locksmith's help the next morning.

Early in the morning, Heidi said to me, "I've got to get you out of here 'cause I'm leaving Johnny today."

"Why would you do a thing like that?" I asked in amazement. I then sat down with her and shared with her some of the principles in the book I was writing, and challenged her to see if they would work in her marriage.

Later, Heidi shared with me:

Talking with you, Gary, was the beginning of having any ray of hope that God could rebuild the ruins of my broken-down marriage. That night I made the commitment to give it a year. But looking back, I realize that it wasn't until I made the decision that divorce was not an option, that I really began to work on the relationship. Over the next few weeks, however, as I struggled to apply the relational principles you taught, I realized I didn't have the fullness of God's power to accomplish my goal of winning back my husband.

So I began to proactively seek God's Word. I used to require a great deal of sleep. Johnny was so controlling that if he went to bed he wanted me there with him. I would wait until everyone was asleep. Then sometimes it would take me several minutes to crawl out of bed because I'd inch out so I wouldn't wake Johnny up. To make matters worse, we had an old house, so there were these loud "creaking" noises as I tried to tiptoe down the stairs. Johnny would yell out, "Heidi, what are you doing? Get back to bed!" So I began to keep a pillow in my walk-in closet.

In the wee hours of the morning, as soon as I could get him to sleep, I would creep into my closet. I got on the floor with my pillow and my Bible in hand, begging God to provide answers. I literally read two Bibles until the pages were falling out. I've got both of them to this day; these Bibles are great reminders of God's faithfulness. I can just open my Bible and see the tearstained pages.

Furthermore, I would journal what I'd learned in the Word that night. And then I'd try to put it to practice. Then the changes started to happen. The person who once required ten to twelve hours of sleep began to need only six hours, then four hours. There were some nights I stayed up all night begging God for answers.

Unfortunately, the time I spent praying and reading the Bible on the floor of my closet was only part of God's plan for my life and marriage. I still needed to make some behavioral changes. But I still was often doing things that drove us apart. I would get depressed and would fight with Johnny. Or I would dump my feelings and problems on him all at once. He would withdraw from the relationship, seemingly overwhelmed by my emotional outpouring.

One of my "emotional word pictures" was that I felt like a clown at the circus. Remember when they brought out the big barrelful of water, and placed the clown on a board over the barrel? Then someone would try to hit the bull's-eye so the clown would crash into the water. I thought my life was like the clown sitting out there on that board. Johnny was always throwing something at my Achilles' heel—trying to dunk me in a deep barrel of water.

Soon I learned that the more I reached out, the more I felt rejected. I had many emotional needs for my husband to meet and became dependent upon his fulfilling them instead of allowing God to fill my cup. Eventually, I stopped reaching out to Johnny. It now felt as if when Johnny hit the bull's-eye—by saying crushing things to me for example—I couldn't go on. I felt as if I were being dunked into a barrel of alcohol.

The Importance of Prayer

Nothing changes without prayer. The current distance between you and your husband will not change without prayer. You might begin by praying this classic prayer by Evelyn Underhill for acceptance: "Take from me all that hinders and teach me to accept in its place all that You accept: The ceaseless demands, needs, conflicts, pressures, misunderstandings, even of those who love You best."

Heidi prayed. Heidi shared with Greg how prayer helped her and her husband close the distance gap.

In seeking to win my husband back, I learned to be a prayer warrior in the closet and a seeker of the Word. Instead of praying, "Lord, change Johnny," my attitude changed and my heart changed. My heart had to be right before the Lord. It would never happen until my heart was clean before Him. I was a prisoner; a prisoner in a gorgeous house with lovely things all around me. All the antiques and the pretty things don't make a person happy or fulfilled in life. It's only as we live for the Lord Jesus that our lives will ever be fulfilled. We can try every other thing; we can even take the Word of God and try to apply it, but if we don't have the resurrection power of the Holy Spirit, then we cannot live out those truths. It's like getting in the car without any gas. We won't go anywhere if there is no fuel. It takes the fuel of the Holy Spirit to move us in the direction of positive change.

Furthermore, I began to see God helping me win Johnny back in simple ways. Johnny would ask me to do things that in the old days, I would have pitched a royal fit about. The Holy Spirit challenged me to develop a new attitude (Phil. 2).

Then I would surrender to that new attitude. If Johnny wanted me to do something I didn't want to do, instead of pitching a fit, I would do it. As I became a servant to my husband, it reminded me of what I read in 1 Peter 3, that we could win our husbands without a word. Instead we could win them by our behavior and a gentle, quiet spirit.

And there wasn't anything quiet about me. One of the verses talked about Sarah's pure heart. I needed a pure heart to be obedient, not for Johnny's sake, not even to win him back, but to honor the Lord Jesus. As I began to live before Johnny with my eyes fixed on the Lord instead of myself or Johnny, he began to see major changes in my life. Then, as Johnny began to see the changes, he said, "I would sit at my office, thinking up things that I knew you would not do for me. I then would go home and challenge you to do them. I would just sit back and watch to see how you would respond. Time and time again, you shocked me by your actions. I slowly began to fall in love with the new person you were becoming. Less argumentative, less dependent, stronger, and most important, happier."

God was truly working in both of their lives.

Abandon prayerlessness. When you are feeling bad about your marriage or yourself, you will be tempted not to pray. You might say to yourself, "What good will it do? Nothing will help. Everything is so futile and hopeless." Such attacks from the enemy of your soul will discourage you and rob you of joy and hope.

Praying for your marriage will be one of the most powerful and effective tools you have in winning your husband back. Note our paraphrase of Paul's words in Ephesians 6:18:

"Pray at all times, even when you don't feel like it, and on every occasion, even on the bad days when your marriage is in the pits, in the power of the Holy Spirit, not your own strength. Stay alert to what's happening between you and your husband and be persistent in your prayers—don't quit or give up—for all Christians everywhere—especially yourself and your husband—whether he's more distant or closer than ever."

Be accountable in your prayer life. The best way to stay consistent in prayer is to have prayer partners to pray with and for you regularly. In the process of communicating with your husband, you may also try praying together. Start simply. Pray Psalm 23 or Numbers 6:24–26 over one another. Pray blessing and encouragement for one another. Keep a prayer list for each other. Here are fifty simple ways to pray with each other. Circle the ones that might be most effective in bringing you and your husband closer together:

1. Pray and read and meditate on or memorize Scripture together.
2. Pray loudly together.
3. Have daily devotions together.
4. Write down your prayers for and with each other.
5. Keep a spiritual journal together.
6. Pray silently together.
7. Pray in the car together while driving to your destination.
8. Sing your prayers together.
9. Recite daily your blessings and God's answers to your prayers.
10. Use a concordance to search the Scriptures for . . .

- all the promises of God.
- all the prayers in the Bible.
- all the verses about prayer in the Bible.
- all the times God answered prayer in the Bible.

11. Read a Christian book together, taking turns reading to each other.
12. Pray together in a worship service.
13. Pray together while taking a walk.
14. Pray together after making love.
15. Keep a prayer list for the needs of others and pray over it regularly.
16. Keep a list of each other's prayer needs and freely add to one another's list. Remember to give praise when prayers are answered.
17. Join a prayer group or go to a prayer service or concert of prayer together.
18. Write prayers for one another and share them.
19. Find a book of prayers in your Christian bookstore and pray through it together.
20. Take a prayer retreat together.
21. Pray and fast together one day, one week, or even longer.
22. Confess your sins to one another daily.
23. Make a praise list and pray through it.
24. Lay hands on one another and pray for one another.
25. Pray in the Spirit for one another.
26. Do spiritual mapping of your community or region and pray down strongholds together.
27. Anoint one another with oil and pray for healing.
28. Pack prayer requests in one another's clothing when you travel.

29. Call each other during the day and pray for each other over the phone.
30. Find a spiritually mature couple and ask them to share ways they pray together and grow spiritually closer.
31. Ask your pastor to pray a blessing over you.
32. Go to the elders together for anointing with oil and prayer.
33. Spend time together praying at the altar of your church.
34. Visit your neighbors and ask how you might pray for them.
35. Pray for Christian leaders together—teachers, missionaries, pastors, youth workers, preachers, prophets, etc.
36. Pray over each other's ears, mouths, and eyes to protect what is taken into each other's lives.
37. Turn the television or radio off and pray.
38. Replace your favorite weekly television program with prayer.
39. Go on a prayer date instead of out to dinner or some other recreational activity.
40. Take pictures of those you are praying for and write prayers on the backs of their pictures.
41. Write prayer notes or letters to each other and mail them.
42. Write down all the things you are thankful for in your spouse and then pray through that list in their hearing.
43. Pray together before each meal.
44. Set a time each day when you will pray with each other and for each other if you work apart.
45. Ask your children to pray for the two of you together.

46. Kneel down before your mate and pray over their feet crying out for God's mercy and guidance.
47. Pray the same way over your spouse's mind and hands.
48. Pray together for the lost. List the lost people you know and pray for their salvation naming each one in your prayer.
49. Sit silently together listening for God's voice and sharing what He says to each of you.
50. Take a fixed interval of time—five minutes, one hour, twenty-four hours, or any interval you choose—and pray continually with one another during that time.

You might be interested to know that Johnny and Heidi have had a wonderful marriage for many years now. God not only restored their marriage but has given them an effective ministry to other couples struggling and needing hope. We know of no other couple who have more faith and belief that God can do anything through prayer. The key came first for Heidi when she decided to "look in the mirror" and ask God to change what and whom she saw before restoring their marriage.

An essential key to winning your husband back has nothing to do with him and everything to do with you. Now it's time for you to look at yourself in the mirror!

Chapter . . . .
Three . . . .

Looking in the Mirror . . . Become Whole

I met with a sort of people that held women have no souls, adding, in a light manner, no more than a goose. But I reproved them, and told them that was not right; for Mary said, "My soul doth magnify the Lord, and my spirit hath rejoiced in God my Saviour."

—George Fox, *Journal, I*

Debbie's husband was staying late at the office and then attending out-of-town business meetings on a regular basis without her. Finally the truth emerged that he was having an affair. After many angry confrontations, he decided to move out. Here is what happened in her own words:

> That day is still fresh in my mind. "I'm moving out today!" my husband, Robert, announced in a cold, distant voice. "They're delivering a bed to my apartment in a few hours. I'll be back later to pick up my clothes and other personal belongings." And with that, Robert was gone.

I stood there looking bewildered. There were so many things I wanted to say to make him stay. There were so many things that I wanted to say to make him pay. After all, he was the one who had had the affair. But most of all, I just wanted my marriage to work out.

With that in mind, the only thing I managed to say was, "Fine." I had to go to work that day knowing that when I came home my husband would no longer be living there.

The rest of our separation is not as clearly etched in my mind as the day Robert left. We spent a period where he lived alone in the city. But during this time he would call me or show up and we would have "dates." We would try to reconcile. We would get along really well, but then I would find out he was still seeing this other woman. Then we'd have a huge fight and he'd be back to his place in the city. I would be left wondering if this was the final straw that would break the back of our marriage.

We cycled through this dance for about a year. Yet, I believe several positive things happened during that year—especially for me as a person. For example, I got a new job and spent time cultivating several deep friendships. These things helped establish my own identity as an individual. I was beginning to feel stronger and better able to be alone. But then Robert would show up or would set up a time for us to be together. We would fall right back in step with our relational dance. We would argue because I knew that he had just been with her. So I was consistently angry and irritable because I felt like I was being repeatedly betrayed. This was our dance.

Looking back on that time, I can see that I did many things to compromise my own self. I did a lot of card sending, phone calling, and tried being the perfect cook when we were together. To be more physically attractive, I lost weight and frequented the local tanning salon. I can remember thinking, *Well, this may be good for him but it's definitely not good for me.* But I came to the conclusion that something first had to be good for me—my self-image and self-esteem—before it could be good for us relationally. If I was miserable, then I would never be able to build a satisfying relationship with my husband.

Ultimately, I learned that weight loss and exercise should be done for my health, not just for my appearance or to win back my man. I also learned that I needed to develop my own interests and learn how to take care of myself financially. Thus, I gained self-esteem knowing that I could work and support myself.

The bottom line was that I became tired of trying to please Robert by being the "perfect" wife—like the ones in the movies and magazines. I finally started leaving him alone. Over time, we started to communicate some. We even began to learn about our most basic relational needs. I feel that this marked the turning point in our relationship.

As Debbie began taking care of herself and becoming the whole person God had created her to be, she looked at the positives in herself and in her marriage. With that change in attitude, her relationship with her husband also began to improve. After a season of dating and focusing on the positives, here's what happened:

Robert moved back into our home after almost one year of counseling and learning new relationship skills. We are still on the journey toward having a satisfying marriage. In winning back my husband, the greatest thing I've learned is the importance of understanding my own needs and the needs of others, not just my husband's needs. Learning to meet my own needs was a major factor in bridging the gap in our marital distance.

Debbie began to build her new relationship with her husband on a new foundation—focusing on the positive and becoming whole. Just as you wouldn't think of building a new house on an old, faulty foundation, don't build a new marital relationship on an old you. Your life is built on the rock of Jesus Christ. In Christ, you are a new creation—body, soul, and spirit.

Taking Care of Yourself to Win Back Your Husband

Winning your husband back starts with you. Yes, he may need to change, but the first one to change should be you. Yes, he may have said and done many hurtful things. But, you must first identify and take responsibility for your own actions, words, thoughts, and feelings. Unless you begin with you and the changes you need to make, you will continue to do and say things that will drive your husband farther away. Winning your husband back begins with you. Recognize who you are in Christ. With beauty and grace, God has created and fashioned you. You are fearfully and wonderfully made.

Also recognize who your husband is in Christ. As believers, you are royalty, priests, and saints of the Most High. God's bringing you together as one in Christ is no mistake or accident. He has a wonderful plan and purpose for your life as a woman as well as a wife.

Hear God say to you: "For I know the plans I have for you," says the LORD. "They are plans for good and not for disaster, to give you a future and a hope. In those days when you pray, I will listen. If you look for me in earnest, you will find me when you seek me."[1]

If your sole purpose for reading this book is to win your husband back, you may end up very disappointed. But if your purpose is to become more of the person God created you to be in Christ, more of the child of God you are born again to be, then you will grow, mature, and overcome an obstacle in life including the possibility that your husband may not return.

You are not seeking a cosmetic, superficial relationship with a returning husband. Because you belong to Christ, you need a marriage in which both of you know that you are called to be one in Christ. Anything less will only be a temporary reconciliation. True reunion comes when both wife and husband see themselves and one another as Christ sees them.

You are growing in Christ to be a godly woman who depends on Christ, not on a husband. If both of you join ranks to depend on Christ, then your reunion and reconciliation have lasting potential and possibility. But if you try to win your husband back before you are secure in your identity in Christ, then you will ultimately lose both your husband and your unique worth in Christ.

In Christ you will be successful at the end of this journey when you can say, "I am unique in Christ. I am myself—holy, redeemed, and acceptable to Jesus, my Lord and Savior."

You cannot change your husband; only God can do that. You can yield to God at work in you for change and new growth. You cannot guarantee that taking all the right steps naturally and spiritually will win your husband back. But you can be assured that as you mature in Christ, you will be prepared and equipped to walk through every future circumstance you will face in marriage or outside marriage. You can't control what will happen, but you can control your obedience to God's Word. Make a decision to first succeed in Christ as His child. Only then is there a possibility for success in marriage.

Winning your husband back begins with you, not with him. It begins with . . .

- seeing yourself through the Bridegroom's eyes, not the groom's eyes.
- acceptance and forgiveness, not condemnation.
- refusing to let the past become your future.
- releasing unresolved anger.
- making a plan founded on God's wisdom and guidance, not feelings and opinions.

As you become more and more the person Christ created you to be, you will become more attractive and beautiful to your husband. The Christ in you will attract the Christ in him. Your indwelling Spirit will transform you from the inside out. Winning your husband back involves more than changing your attitudes or behaviors—even though they may have to change substantially. The change in you is a spiritual transformation out of which flows new life through you and into your marriage relationship.

You are not treating your husband as the old wife did, you are treating him as Christ does. You are not loving him as you used to love him, but you are loving him with the love of Christ. How is that possible? Because your identity is rooted in Christ, you do not see your identity as simply a role or a fulfillment of your husband's expectations.

Ask yourself these questions:

What is God's design for me?
How did God create me?
What is His calling on my life?
What is my uniqueness as a person?
What is God's good plan and purpose for my life?

In the last chapter, we focused on allowing Christ to fill your life. We also learned about the power of prayer. Now we are asking you to focus on yourself. It's time to look at yourself in the mirror. To see yourself inside and out. Don't even think about what is happening in your husband's life or about his strengths or weaknesses. This chapter is all about you. It's about seeing yourself the way you really are and becoming excited about your future in Christ.

We have chosen an actual letter that is an example of the hundreds of letters our ministry receives. As you read this letter, note how often Kate refers to her husband, Bob, and how rarely she steps back to look at herself.

My husband, Bob, and I have been to a counselor three times, but all she told us was to get a lawyer. After twenty-five years of marriage and a deep love for my husband, that is the last thing I want to do. Bob has watched some of your relationship videos with me, but I can't see that it has made any difference. What we need to do is very clear, but he won't commit to anything. Please help me. I have lost thirty-five pounds, tried to commit suicide, and my general well-being is fragile. Everyone tells me to divorce him and find someone who will appreciate me. I love my husband and I want to do everything I can to put our marriage back on track. I'm really trying to bury my anger and hurt feelings but it is so hard.

Over the last year my husband admitted to having an affair. He claims he tried to be intimate with me, but to him intimacy was in bed. I had my own hang-ups about sex and I needed more than just the act of sex. I needed him to care about me first. He has never told me he needed me or wanted me to stay. On the other hand, he says he still loves me and always will.

I know if we could spend time together and truly work on things our problems could be reversed. Our daughter graduates this summer. He seems afraid to try and make a life with just the two of us because circumstances have kept us apart. I know I have made a lot of mistakes, but I always wanted our life to be together forever. I want grandchildren one day, and the kids to bring their kids home to see Grandpa and Grandma. I want to grow old with the man I said I would love, honor, and cherish. Gary, it's not fair! I thought I did what he wanted me to. I raised the kids and stayed out of his way. Now he claims I never wanted to do anything with him.

I want to turn this situation around before it does permanent damage. I want to live, but I'm afraid I'm losing the battle. Every day is a struggle. I know I'm not hopeless or helpless, and every time I get close to doing something stupid I watch your tapes or read your books. Right now you are my lifesaver, literally.

Notice that her focus is almost exclusively on her husband, Bob. She is willing to lose herself and her identity for the marriage and assumes that she is the reason for their marital distance. Kate needs to do something very simple: become whole. It's time for her to look at herself as a wonderful person whom God created to be loved and cherished, not treated as an accessory in life by her husband. John affirms, "But as many as received him, to them gave he power to become the sons of God, even to them that believe on his name."[2] You are becoming like Christ. Becoming through the process of growing and maturing.

Barriers to Wholeness

As you enter the process of becoming the "whole" person God intends for you to be, there can be several things that interfere. These things can act as barriers, keeping you from reaching your potential. When remodeling a house, things like poor weather, insufficient funds, and the lack of a plan can interfere with successful completion. Likewise, there are three negative issues that can hinder the journey toward winning back your husband.

1. *Being too needy or dependent.* Author Stephen Covey uses the word *interdependent.* This word simply means that a person is neither too dependent on nor too independent of another person. Interdependent, instead, is the balance point between these two extremes. We often refer to indi-

viduals as being dependent on their mate as one cause of marital problems. But marital difficulties arise when someone functions too independently of his or her mate as well. Both extremes can lead a couple to the same point: relational misery.

But let us focus on the dependent side of the continuum at this point. When a person becomes overly dependent on his or her mate, it can often lead to the other person feeling overwhelmed, leeched onto, fatigued, or confined. We heard one husband describe his wife's dependency as feeling like "a scuba diver with my own tank of air strapped onto my back. Instead of my wife having her own air tank, she continually grabs the emergency mouth piece from my tank to breathe. The problem is that my air tank has only enough air to support me. She is literally sucking the life out of me. I feel like I have to swim away just to survive."

Carrie shared with us her battle with dependency.

One day I started praying and taking full responsibility in our relationship for things in my life. I quit heaping all this blame for our problems onto my husband. I also stopped looking at him to satisfy all my needs. Over time, it seemed that our relationship started to improve. But that required me to leave it alone and become my own person.

Even though my husband was wrong for what he was doing, I just started taking responsibility for the things that I was doing. When a friend told me that I was entirely too needy, a little gong went off, and I started to see that maybe it was true. I needed another woman to tell me that. Then I started asking, "How can I be less needy? How can I take care of some of this myself instead of being such a blamer and looking for him to fulfill all this stuff and to solve all these problems?"

Regardless of where the faults lie for the breakdown of your marriage, you must take ownership of your life and responsibility for the things that you need to change. If your husband is having or has had an affair, you cannot let your life and identity depend on whether or not he returns to you. Decide to say, "I belong to Christ and He has given me the strength to depend on no one but Him." Dependency on your husband will never win him back; it can only drive him farther away.

If you are too dependent on your husband, decide to become Christ-dependent. Stop looking for a groom who can never meet the needs that only the Bridegroom, Jesus, can meet. Say to yourself, "I am a unique person in Christ." Your husband will never see that uniqueness until you do.

2. Blaming factors outside the marriage for failure in your marriage. Our friend Dr. Gary Oliver remarked, "The problem with the blame response is that it robs us of the opportunity to identify and take responsibility for our part of the problem. If we miss that step, we're also going to miss what God wants to teach us. And if we allow that to happen, we've really failed. We've turned the situation into a double loss."[3]

Blaming your in-laws, another woman, your husband's job, or other factors for your marriage's failures only increases distance between you and your husband. Blame actually paralyzes you from taking responsible actions to win your husband back.

The key to overcoming blame is to take ownership. Own the parts of the failures or problems for which you are responsible. Take your focus off other things and people and put it on yourself.

Let's return to our home renovation analogy. If we are remodeling the kitchen, we cannot focus on fixing all the problems in the den and hope to get anywhere in the kitchen. If we start worrying about the den every time we start working in the kitchen, we will never get the kitchen remodeled. Likewise, focusing on your husband, other people, or other situations does not help you change.

Your husband may be violating your boundaries, but you may have never set the boundaries in the first place. So you blame him for invasion, but he fails to understand what he has done wrong. You become unhappy with him because you have chosen to be unhappy, not because he intends to cross your boundaries and hurt you. Yes, he may be doing and saying many hurtful things in the marriage. But you cannot change him—you can only change yourself.

The issue is blame versus ownership. Will you own the part of the problem that is yours or will you sidestep responsibility and blame others for your failures in marriage?

3. Letting the way your parents raised you determine how you relate to your husband. Your parents may have given you one set of role models for husbands and wives while your husband grew up with a completely different set of role models. How your parents emotionally and physically treated you as a child deeply affects how you treat others, especially your mate.

If your parents were abusive to one another or to you, you will have a tendency to be abusive to your spouse and children. One of the main reasons why adult parents tend to "parent" as their own parents did is because the deep anger can be transferred from one generation to another. It's long-standing anger that makes us behave in absusive ways.

Likewise, if your parents were affectionate and affirming to one another and you, then you will have a positive role model for how to treat your husband and children.

You are not trapped by the way you were raised. The past does not determine your future. The Scripture promises, "What this means is that those who become Christians become new persons. They are not the same anymore, for the old life is gone. A new life has begun!"[4]

Since you have a new life in Christ, you are your Father's child, not your parents' child. So is your husband. Decide to affirm who you are in Christ and to affirm the same characteristics in your husband. Here is who you and your husband truly are in Christ:

Scripture	Who You and Your Husband Are in Christ
Genesis 1:26–27	Created in God's image
Matthew 5:13, 14	The salt and light of the world
John 1:12	A child of God
Romans 5:1	Not condemned by God
1 Corinthians 3:9	God's fellow worker and His building
1 Corinthians 3:16, 17; 6:19	The temple of the Holy Spirit
2 Corinthians 5:17	A new person in Christ
2 Corinthians 4:16	A renewed person daily
Philemon 6	One filled with the knowledge of every good thing
1 Peter 2:9, 10	A chosen race, a royal priest, and a citizen of a holy nation

This list is only a brief summary of the hundreds of wonderful attributes you and your husband have in Christ. See yourself and your husband as God sees you. His perspective of you is the only one that counts for eternity.

Becoming Whole

Imagine trying to rebuild or remodel your home with all the doors and windows locked. If there were no way to get into the house, you could never change or renovate anything. Likewise, old role models and perspectives, especially negative ones inherited from your parents, will shut the door and lock it when you try to win your husband back. But when you and your husband strongly hold God's declaration of who He created you to be, the door will open to winning your husband back.

God's view of you is like throwing away dark, musty drapes from an old house, opening the windows, and letting warm, bright light bathe the whole house with gleaming golden sunlight. Let His light shine on your perspectives of one another!

Let's return to our house remodeling examples. In some homes there is a room that is rarely used. It may be a spare bedroom, office, or sitting room. This room may not be essential to the family's lifestyle. In a real estate listing, it may be labeled as a bonus room. Some women view themselves as "bonus rooms" in their husbands' lives. They accept the role that their husbands let them play. They are "extras" in their husbands' movies!

If you are feeling this way, let me assure you that God has a wonderful plan and purpose for your life even if your husband doesn't see you as important or essential to his life. You are body, soul, and spirit. *All* of who you are is important to God. We will examine each aspect of your life and look at how you can become whole regardless of how your husband views you. All that matters is that you see yourself as God sees you.

The Bible says that we are body, soul, and spirit, "Now may the God of peace make you holy in every way, and may your whole spirit and soul and body be kept blameless until that day when our Lord Jesus Christ comes again."[5] So let's look in the mirror at the whole person—body, soul, and spirit.

Once you touch the saving and healing power of Jesus Christ, you are made whole: ". . . and as many as touched him were made whole."[6]

You are a whole person reflecting Christ's image, not the image projected for you by your husband, others, or even yourself. So let's look at you as God does.

Look at Your Body

The way you look physically may convey to others how you feel about yourself. A sloppy, overweight person can communicate that he or she is expressing a belief of lower self-value. There could be several reasons why a person is "sloppy" or overweight. If in your case, you have a hard time losing weight, it could be from how you were raised, or something genetic or medical in nature. But if it's none of those, you may be surprised by the results of a great program to help men and women lose the weight they desire. It's called the "Weigh Down Workshop." The essence of the program is to set your main focus on Christ and let Him "fill" your heart. Food is something that fills the stomach, not the spirit. Some people try to use food to fill their empty spirit. Your body is also the temple of the Holy Spirit. "Don't you know that your body is the temple of the Holy Spirit, who lives in you and was given to you by God? You do not belong to yourself."[7]

It's important for you to take care of your body for your sake and so that you can be a healthy vessel through whom the Spirit works.

Remember that your body's greatest enemies are lack of sleep and improper nutrition. When combined, they put you under constant stress and leave you irritable. Such a state of body would not make you attractive to your husband or anyone else for that matter.

One obvious way to solve the problem of fatigue, listlessness, and irritability is regular, vigorous exercise. Stay fit. Commit yourself to a regular routine of exercise. Consider these options not only for yourself but also for winning your husband back:

- Jogging
- Bicycling
- An exercise class
- Working out at a health spa
- Setting up a regular walking or swimming routine
- A checkup and a physical

Of course, be certain to consult a physician if you have any health problems that may restrict your exercise. Keep your body fit in order to honor the Lord, to be used by Him for His purposes, and to stay attractive to your husband and others. But you are not doing this to look good or to win your husband back. This is for your health and for God.

Look at Your Soul

Next, it's important to cultivate and maintain a healthy mental outlook. The hymn intones, "Jesus, lover of my soul." John writes, "Beloved, I wish above all things that thou mayest prosper and be in health, even as thy soul prospereth."[8]

A healthy soul begins with Christ's thoughts, which focus on the positive not the negative things in life. Paul writes, "Fix your thoughts on what is true and honorable and right. Think about things that are pure and lovely and admirable. Think about things that are excellent and worthy of praise."[9]

The mind of Christ in you cannot be filled with criticism or judgmental attitudes toward your husband. When you find yourself beginning to argue, follow these general guidelines so that you will reflect the mind of Christ:

- Remove the blame from your comments.
- Say how you feel.
- Don't criticize your partner's personality.
- Don't insult, mock, or use sarcasm.
- Be direct.
- Stick with one situation.
- Don't try to analyze your partner's personality.
- Don't mind-read.

Since Jesus is the lover of your soul, how can you genuinely love yourself and your husband the way God loves you? Look at yourself in the mirror—are you a lover or a complainer . . . a lover or a judge . . . a lover or a critic?

What attitudes do you have toward yourself? Look at the list below. Circle the attitudes of your soul and then go back and underline the attitudes you have toward marriage.

Hopeful	Depressed	Expectant	Anxious	Nervous
Worried	Loving	Angry	Bitter	Peaceful
Critical	Affirming	Accepting	Judgmental	Pure

If you found yourself circling or underlining more negative than positive attitudes, it's time to do a serious soul realignment. Decide to put on the mind of Christ and to set aside negative attitudes that serve to damage you and your relationships.

Examine your soul for balance. Answer these questions:

- Do you have a social life with other women friends?
- What are your hobbies?
- What's the best book you have read lately?
- Are your friends positive people who affirm and encourage you?
- Do you have time for serving and ministering to others?
- What new ways are you learning and growing intellectually?
- If you spend a lot of time with children each day, how are you spending time for yourself?

Time for yourself is important in a daily schedule. Make yourself and your attitudes a priority for your time.

Look at Your Spirit

Now it's time to examine your spiritual life. What are you doing to feed the spiritual dimension of your personality? You feed your spirit with Scripture. Jesus assures us, "It is the Spirit who gives eternal life. Human effort accomplishes nothing. And the very words I have spoken to you are spirit and life."[10]

It's also important to look at any unconfessed sin in your life that may be blocking your relationship with God. Imagine again the house that we have talked about redecorating. You might have a room that is dark and windowless. In order for that room to really come alive with vibrant color, you will need a window. It may be necessary for you to knock a hole in the wall and put in a window. As light floods the room, darkness flees.

Likewise, the darkness of unconfessed sin can block the light and joy of Christ in your life. Paul writes, "For though your hearts were once full of darkness, now you are full of light from the Lord, and your behavior should show it! For this light within you produces only what is good and right and true. Try to find out what is pleasing to the Lord."[11]

One of the darkest and most forbidding rooms in any heart is that of unforgiveness. When you do not forgive yourself, your spouse, or others, a thick wall is constructed in your spirit between you and God. Jesus warns, "If you forgive those who sin against you, your heavenly Father will forgive you. But if you refuse to forgive others, your Father will not forgive your sins."[12]

One couple shared with us about their struggle with unforgiveness. Forgiveness was a major issue because she was unwilling to forgive because of the deep hurt she had experienced. The level of trust in the relationship had deteriorated. Due to mistrust and pride, she was unable to forgive him. We finally counseled her, "If you hold on to that, it is going to make you unhappy. Forgiveness is going to restore joy to your relationship."

Spiritual wholeness involves becoming like Jesus. The popular cliché asks, "What would Jesus do?" Jesus always forgives. He has unconditional love for others. And you must forgive yourself. If God forgives you, why do you still put yourself under condemnation? Paul wrote, "So now there is no condemnation for those who belong to Christ Jesus. For the power of the life-giving Spirit has freed you through Christ Jesus from the power of sin that leads to death."[13]

You may be filled with shame and condemnation if you were the one having an affair. Forgiveness begins with your repentance to God and His forgiving you. Then you must forgive yourself. Don't wait until your husband forgives you. He may not yet be spiritually mature enough to forgive. But your forgiveness doesn't depend on his forgiving you. It starts with you appropriating the forgiveness and love that God has for you and receiving His forgiveness. Forgiveness is a critical spiritual step.

If there is unforgiveness in your spirit, take these steps now:

- Repent and accept God's forgiveness.
- Love and forgive others unconditionally.
- Refuse to live under condemnation.

As a new creation in Christ, you are a whole person. Your wholeness depends on who you are in Christ, not who you have been or who others think you are. Commit to implementing these steps toward wholeness:

- Stay fit and healthy.
- Keep a daily routine of exercise and proper nutrition.

- Put on the mind of Christ.
- Maintain healthy, positive attitudes toward yourself, others, and your husband.
- Stay accountable to prayer partners and a spiritual mentor.
- Develop encouraging friendships with others.
- Grow intellectually. Take time for yourself every day.
- Spend time daily in the Scriptures and prayer.
- Decide to forgive yourself and others as God forgives.
- Be the whole person God has created you to be in the image of Christ.

You cannot win your husband back alone. And regardless of all the changes and growth within you, you need others to help you. It's time to get support.

Chapter Four

Get Support!

Two are better than one because they have a good return for their labor. For if either of them falls, the one will lift up his companion. But woe to the one who falls when there is not another to lift him up. Furthermore, if two lie down together they keep warm, but how can one be warm alone? And if one can overpower him who is alone, two can resist him. A cord of three strands is not quickly torn apart.

—Ecclesiastes 4:9–12 NASB

Rick was always busy. When he wasn't working late, he would become involved in community organizations, training seminars, and civic clubs. He overcommitted himself. Brenda responded initially by becoming more involved herself with the children and things outside the marriage. Deep inside, she knew they were drifting apart, but she felt that Rick just didn't have time for her. Out of anger and neglect, she developed the attitude, "If that's [being too busy for marriage] what he wants, then he can do what he likes. I'll just do my own thing as well."

Brenda tried to repress and deny her needs for closeness and intimacy. She felt that if she shared with Rick anything about her feelings or family problems, it would simply overload him. But there came the day when all the repression and denial failed to keep the lid on the pressure cooker of Brenda's inner feelings of anger, hurt, and frustration. She resolved to pull Rick back into the marriage and family before all the children were grown and "life had passed them by." Brenda's plan to rebuild the house of their marriage relationship took shape.

Brenda's plan was built on attack! Remember how Brenda remarked in the introduction that she and her husband had grown apart due to busyness? The more overcommitted Rick became at work and in community organizations, the more Brenda withdrew in the relationship, allowing him to do whatever he wanted.

Rick became bogged down with more and more stuff to accomplish, but none of it involved his family or marriage. Brenda became angry that her needs were not being met, and at the same time, she felt guilty that she couldn't meet Rick's needs—and didn't want to!

A few years passed as the volcano of molten anger grew under the unstable cap of repressed expectations and unmet needs. A seismic explosion was simmering just under the surface of civility when Brenda could contain herself no longer.

In their daughter's senior year of high school, Brenda finally realized that intimate time with their daughter was rapidly coming to an end with her graduation and plans to go off to school. Rick had missed too many opportunities to be with her and at her activities.

"Rick, you're always gone," Brenda attacked. "And we're not building memories with the children."

As could be expected, Rick's reaction was defensive denial. "I'm the one who is providing for this family. Do you think money ends up in our bank account by osmosis?"

Brenda discovered that the more she harped, nagged, and attacked, the farther Rick ran away from marriage and family. Rick didn't just emotionally distance himself from Brenda or leave the house for a while, he would find more things to do and new ways to keep busy away from Brenda and the children. Needless to say, Brenda's attack plan didn't work. She wasn't winning her husband back, she was driving him farther away.

Brenda expected Rick to listen to her needs and then to help her get those needs met. But her plan was faulty. Finally she found herself needing to put together a new blueprint for winning her husband back. She needed a new plan. She needed support.

You Need Support

You cannot win your husband back by yourself. You need God's help and the help of others. Find a friend or a small group of friends. Look to someone older than yourself. Find a mentor who has been through a similar experience and now has a loving, godly marriage.

If you were building or rebuilding a home, you couldn't start working on the dining room or redecorating the den if there was no foundation to the house. Your marriage right now is like a house with walls and a roof on but no foundation for support. What do you do if the house is already built but the foundation is cracked? Find people around you to help you reform and reset a right foundation for your life. You need mentors who will help you get the foundation right.

When you seek out mentors, carefully choose those people who will help you, not just sympathize with your problems. What you don't need are people who will agree with you about how terrible your husband or your circumstances are. Negative people will not lift you up. They can only pull you down. You need to build a foundation, not destroy one.

What kind of people do you need for support? In the New Testament, Paul describes these mentors as older women. "These older women must train the younger women to love their husbands and their children, to live wisely and be pure, to take care of their homes, to do good, and to be submissive to their husbands. Then they will not bring shame on the word of God."[1] Here are some important qualities to look for in older women who would mentor you:

Mentors pray for and with you. At the beginning of this chapter, we told the story about Brenda's initial plan of attacking her husband. It didn't work. As things grew worse in their relationship, she realized that she didn't know how to win her husband back. She needed help. And she found that help and support through women who would listen to her and pray and study the Bible with her. Brenda commented, "Women need other women friends. Women need a Bible study and prayer partners or a small group for supporting one another. Other women do not substitute for my husband, but no husband can meet all of his wife's needs. She needs friends to help test reality and discover truth."

A mentor is there for you. One of the greatest battles you will fight in winning your husband back is loneliness. Loneliness often paints a distorted picture of reality. On a canvas of self-pity and depression, loneliness tints everything gray and black, bleak and hopeless, sad and morose. You need someone there who has crossed the valley and reached the other side.

When we fly in overcast skies with low cloud cover, we enjoy the breakthrough that comes from dreariness to sunlit, clear blue skies as the plane rises above the clouds. A mentor is one who can help you navigate from showers to sunshine because they know the way. Left alone you would spend days on end in an overcast mood, filled with gray thoughts.

Someone who is "there for you" cares enough to be there when you call and to come over to "check in" with you when you are lonely. Just being there is a high calling from the Lord who commends those who visit the imprisoned. No prison is more impenetrable than loneliness. A mentor helps you keep the door of loneliness unlocked.

A mentor encourages you. Such a mentor knows the awesome power of being a Barnabas. "For instance, there was Joseph, the one the apostles nicknamed Barnabas (which means "Son of Encouragement"). He was from the tribe of Levi and came from the island of Cyprus."[2] A Barnabas is one who comes alongside you to encourage, affirm, and accept you where you are. Mentors do not have you carry the baggage of guilt, condemnation, or regret. Even though you have experienced some failure in marriage, mentors do not regard you or your marriage as a failure.

A mentor listens. Anyone can give you advice, but only a wise mentor knows when to listen. A mentor is "quick to listen, slow to speak, and slow to get angry."[3] Listening is a gift of time in which the listener conveys acceptance and worth upon another person by simply being willing to hear the cry of a broken heart. Listening helps to ease the pain caused by separation or distance in marriage and provides a release for buried hurts and piercing emotions.

Jesus listened to the hurting Samaritan woman at the well and the distraught Gentile woman who brought her daughter to Him for healing. He listened to all kinds of people with every imaginable problem and disease. There's healing power in listening. Seek out someone who will listen.

A mentor points to truth and reality. A mentor can help you test reality and apply the truths of Scripture to your attitudes, words, and actions. An older woman will share with you her experience of applying God's truths to marital relationships. She will be a source of wisdom and truth.

With truth comes freedom from the past, from guilt, from self-condemnation and hopelessness. The reality of God's truth in your circumstances will free you to begin winning your husband back. Jesus simply asserted, "And you will know the truth, and the truth will set you free."[4]

A few final observations are in order about mentors. First, family mentors rarely make good mentors. They are often too emotionally entangled in your situation to be of much help to you. Other family members have often formed opinions about your marital circumstances and those opinions cloud their perceptions of reality.

It's also difficult for family members to keep confidential those private matters you share with them. A mentor needs to be someone with whom you can trust your deepest feelings and thoughts.

Finally, family members, especially parents or siblings, are prone to give advice instead of godly wisdom. They may often try to give you advice on how to "fix" your marriage or "fix" your husband or yourself instead of sharing with you God's wisdom for your situation.

Get Intercessors

In addition to mentors, we encourage you to elicit another kind of specific help. Have some people that you trust begin praying and interceding for you. These can be trustworthy friends who have no need to know the intimate details of your situation but who will pray for you and your marriage. They only need to know the general situation. The power of prayer is asserted continuously in Scripture. Jesus promised, "I also tell you this: If two of you agree down here on earth concerning anything you ask, my Father in heaven will do it for you. For where two or three gather together because they are mine, I am there among them."[5]

God works through prayer. E. M. Bounds often remarked that nothing happens until we pray. Mentors physically stand beside you. Intercessors spiritually stand with you. We have discovered time and time again that when people are interceding for you . . .

- you will feel supernatural strength to endure and go on.
- you will resist the temptation to give up or quit.
- you will begin to receive new ideas and insights into your problems.

- you will encounter others whom God will bring into your path who have godly wisdom to share with you.
- you will experience the forgiving love and acceptance of God and His people in your circumstances.

Jesus makes continual intercession for us at the throne of God. The Bible urges us to pray without ceasing for one another. As God's Spirit leads you, share with intercessors specific needs that you have and then begin to trust God to meet your needs.

Your plan needs to include intercessors. You cannot physically or spiritually go through this time in your marriage alone. Find at least three people who will pray daily for you, your husband, your family, and your marriage. The power and healing of God will be released in your life through intercession.

The Rest of the Story . . .

I (Greg) asked Brenda what she felt the key was to winning back her husband. Here is what she said:

The most important thing I learned through this experience was what a dear friend of mine said. She is really my mentor. She is a very godly woman, and her counsel was well taken. She quite simply voiced: "Quit being so needy."

Her words struck me between the eyes. I hated seeing myself as "needy." As my friend and I talked further, I believe what she was saying was that needy meant telling Rick my problems and expecting him to help me with them, instead of taking those things to Christ and trying to work through them. It's not that we shouldn't communicate our problems, but we don't have to vent every little thing. Rick isn't equipped to handle all of that. He had his own problems to deal with; solving every little thing at home overwhelmed him. I literally talked my husband away.

As I began to apply my friend's insight, things started to change for the better. To this day, I still share problems with Rick. But I try to find a better time. I also try to not whine and complain about the little things.

As a result, I feel it's important for women to seek other women friends. Women need a Bible study or some other experience with other women. We should not expect our husbands to fulfill this need completely. I'm not suggesting that we find a substitute for our husband's support. Instead, it's vital to reap the benefits of cultivating other female relationships.

Having looked at yourself in the mirror and built support, it will still take a great deal of energy to win your husband back. Let's turn to how to energize yourself for this monumental effort.

Chapter
Five

Energize Yourself

And now these three remain: faith, hope and love. But the greatest of these is love.

—1Corinthians 13:13

This verse beautifully describes the essence of the book: *Faith*. First we must reconcile our relationship with Christ and allow Him to fulfill our needs. *Love*. Next we must learn to love ourselves by becoming whole before we can love others—including our mate. *Hope*. Finally, we must never lose hope.

Never Give Up!

In the book *Joy That Lasts*, I (Gary) wrote about one of the most powerful things to be discovered in life. It is found in Luke chapter 18. It's a story about how we should pray for one another. The word picture that Christ uses is of a little widow who never gave up standing in front of a wicked judge. She kept asking every day for protection against people who were stealing from her.

Imagine an unrighteous, wicked judge assigned to a small city in Israel. He has no respect for God or man. He is disgruntled because he would rather be in Rome enjoying pageantry, games, and parties. Instead he's stuck with a bunch of farmers, shepherds, and religious fanatics. Every day people line up to present their grievances to him and he passes judgments according to his mood.

In the line of people stands a widow with no one to look out for her best interests or to protect her. Her situation appears hopeless. Others take advantage of her, but she has no legal rights. Although many view her as helpless, she knows the secret to gaining justice. The first time she presents her petition to the judge, he abruptly dismisses her. But she does not give up. After many days of standing in line, the wicked judge finally gives her protection. "Why did the wicked judge grant this woman her request?" Jesus asked. "Because she wore him down!" Jesus concludes by telling how much more our heavenly Father gives us when we stand in line every day with our prayer requests.

Luke 18:1–8 talks about what we can do during difficult times of reconciliation. Jesus said to listen carefully to the story of this unrighteous judge. He pictures an important truth people need to understand. It was the woman's persistence that brought results. Jesus went on to say, "Shall not God bring about justice for His elect, who cry to Him day and night, and will He delay long over them?"[1]

Like the little old widow lady, we need to persistently stand before the Lord each day—asking if today is the day He will answer our prayers. It's vital to never give up asking the Lord to bring the needed improvements and growth necessary to help in this process. Continue to ask God for the wisdom, insight, and strength to keep going. Never give up!

This has been one of the most powerful things we've learned in life. We can continue to wait upon the Lord until He renews our strength. He will cause us to rise up and fly like eagles, walking and not fainting. Why? Because He will do it in His time. Especially when it's His will. We know that strong, vibrant relationships are His will. If they aren't true in your marriage, you can continue to pray for these things.

Near the end of his life, Winston Churchill was asked to give a commencement speech at a noted university in England. His car arrived late, and the jam-packed crowd suddenly hushed as one of the greatest men in British history made his way slowly, painfully to the podium. Churchill's speech lasted less than two minutes—but it drew a standing ovation at the time and has inspired decades of men and women ever since. What he said is the best advice you can receive when it comes to being persistent in love, in the face of obstacles.

What did he say? With his deep, resonating voice, he said only these twelve immortal words: "Never give up . . . Never, never give up . . . Never, never, never give up."[2] Then he sat down.

Few can appreciate Churchill's message quite like Tim and Nattalie. For them, "Never give up," means far more than some positive rallying cry or historic speech. It is the testimony of their marriage experience, and one they now feel called to share with others.

For twenty-three years, my husband and I did not have the kind of marriage God intended and only through the pain of divorce did we learn the errors of our ways. There was no adultery or anything like that. In fact, we were admired by many as the perfect Christian family. We have four wonderful sons and good jobs, we have been involved in church activities since 1978 when we accepted Christ as our Lord and Savior. Our children went to Christian school until we could no longer afford to send them, which was another mistake we made.

But the bottom line is we did not love and honor each other. We were committed to everything but each other. Love one another was the end of each day and not the beginning. We gave each other what we had left over and if there was nothing left today, then we hoped for tomorrow, but tomorrow never seemed to come.

I made the mistake of divorcing my husband because in my mind and heart I believed there was no hope for us or for our sons to become good, solid, loving, caring Christian husbands and fathers. I was always trying to make it perfect instead of letting go and letting God.

I am happy to say that we remarried last week after being divorced for 115 days. We will never be the couple we used to be because we have chosen not to be. We are truly blessed by God's unfailing love and patience and most of all His forgiveness.

All of the women we interviewed identified four specific ways to reenergize themselves as they went through the process of winning their husbands back. Think of this journey like being trapped in the middle of the Sahara Desert. With each step you take, the more fatigued and thirsty you become. Sometimes you may feel like collapsing in the sand—too tired to move any farther. Then suddenly you notice an oasis off in the distance. With all your remaining strength you pull yourself to the refreshing water. You shade your sunburned body under the large branches of the surrounding foliage. Instantly, you feel revived—full of energy and added strength. Now you are ready to take on the seemingly endless sand dunes of the marital desert. But now you have been refreshed. Most important, you now possess water bottles overflowing with cool, rejuvenating water to take with you. In the same manner, the following four reenergizers will provide shade and quench your thirst like a lifesaving oasis.

Four Ways to Rejuvenate Yourself

1. *Establish hope.* At this point, you know who you are in Christ. You also accept who your husband is in Christ. You may decide to go into counseling with a pastor or Christian counselor. You have assessed where you are and have determined not to stay there. And you are unwilling to have a quick fix or superficial Band-Aid applied to your marriage. You want a positive change in yourself and are praying for God to work in your husband's life. Others are praying with you. You can even rejoice that through this pain and suffering, you will be personally strengthened and your faith will be refined as pure gold.

God is at work in your marital crisis to form and shape you into the image of Christ. He is transforming you from the inside out. Your character and integrity are being conformed to Christ. You are discovering the truth of which Paul wrote, "We can rejoice, too, when we run into problems and trials, for we know that they are good for us—they help us learn to endure. And endurance develops strength of character in us, and character strengthens our confident expectation of salvation . . . And we know that God causes everything to work together for the good of those who love God and are called according to his purpose for them."[3]

As you become more like Christ, you also begin to act like Him through bearing the fruit of His Spirit—love, joy, peace, patience, kindness, goodness, faithfulness, and self-control. Who wouldn't want to be married to a woman whose life radiated those qualities?

Now we are going to say something that may shock or even offend you at first. But if you need to, take a while to ponder and meditate on this truth: In this dark and very discouraging hour, you have never in your life been in a better place to experience a richer, fuller, and more meaningful relationship with God, yourself, and your husband.

The crisis in which you find yourself is pregnant with possibilities both for you and your marriage. The potential is limitless because the God at work in you is infinite. Right now you are poised to have a relationship with God and in marriage that you have never anticipated. Here's God's promise and my prayer for you:

And I pray that Christ will be more and more at home in your hearts as you trust in him. May your roots go down deep into the soil of God's marvelous love. And may you have the power to understand, as all God's people should, how wide, how long, how high, and how deep his love really is. May you experience the love of Christ, though it is so great you will never fully understand it. Then you will be filled with the fullness of life and power that comes from God. Now glory be to God! By his mighty power at work within us, he is able to accomplish infinitely more than we would ever dare to ask or hope.[4]

In Christ, your situation is full of hope. In a recent movie, *The Truman Show*, there is a particular scene in which the main character, Truman, is sitting on the beach waiting for the sun to rise. He has been through much pain and turmoil, but he finds himself on the verge of making a major life decision. As Truman stares out over the darkened sea, it's as if his whole future, the culmination of all his hopes and dreams, rests upon the sun rising. After all, if he is to have faith that his new decision will produce positive life changes, then the sun must come up. In the midst of great confusion, at least he can count on the sun casting warm, energizing light over his chilled body. As Truman watches with hope-filled eyes, the scene shifts to a man who has been the architect of Truman's invented life. As this man watches Truman's plight, it's as if he understands what his son needs at that moment. And with that, his maker gently commands, "Cue the sunrise." Hope has been granted. In your life, your heavenly Father is "cuing your sunrise" of hope. Keep your eyes focused on Him and His ability to fulfill your needs. Just as Truman discovered, hope is a powerful thing.

2. *Make a commitment.* For years I (Gary) have taught the truth that love is a decision. So is commitment. Committing to love is a decision you make in spite of your feelings. Feelings do not have to precede behavior. You make a commitment to act as if you love your husband whether the feelings of love are there right now or not.

Perhaps you are the one who has been putting distance between you and your husband. You may have been involved in an affair either emotionally or physically. You may still not feel an attraction toward your husband but you can make a decision and a commitment without being attracted right now. The feelings can follow later.

As you make a commitment you need to consider the natural constraints on your commitment. Here are some of those natural constraints:

- Divorce has consequences. With divorce life can become increasingly complicated.
- Children are the broken pieces in divorce. Divorce carries with it hurt, pain, and guilt.
- Divorce is costly. Walking through the financial negotiations and settlement of a divorce is a costly process putting a strain on what may already be a marriage on the financial rocks.
- Divorce hurts children and family. One high school girl illustrated this when she wrote us the following letter.

My name is Jennifer and my parents, Keith and Molly, have been married for almost twenty-five years. I'm sorry to say they haven't been very golden. When I was little (I'm eighteen now) I thought we had a pretty normal family. My brother and I were in 4-H, dance classes, and exploring the land around our house in Texas. My dad manufactured livestock trailers, and my mom stayed at home with us. Sounds fairly normal, don't you think?

I started gymnastics when I was about four and I guess God granted me with talent. My dad was always interested in what my brother and I did, but it seems like even when we were small he hardly had time to come to my competitions or my brother's band concerts. He did make more of an effort then than when we were older. When I was ten we decided to move so I could train in a top-level gym with the best coaches in the area. Quite a dream, but that meant leaving my dad and brother. Not something that seemed real easy to do, but for some strange reason it wasn't that hard, for me anyway.

So it was my mom and me in another city. After a while my brother came to live with us so my dad ended up alone. He came and visited on the weekends, but they went by so fast. I guess you could say we really didn't spend any "quality family time" together. My mom supported me through the sport even though I wanted to quit more than anything at times. After about four years we decided to move. I trained in another city for a while and then finished my gymnastics career in California. My dad moved in with us trying to find a job, but for some reason couldn't land one. So he moved to find employment in another state.

Lately I've been wondering if he really couldn't find a job or if he didn't want a job near us. He traveled back and forth to see us on the weekend. We saw him most every weekend except for this past year.

At the beginning of this year, my senior year, I noticed some changes between my parents. I could tell that they weren't the same around each other. He hardly showed any affection toward my mom. I think the only affection I saw was a hug and maybe a little kiss as he was walking out the door. I'd ask my mom what was wrong and she'd just say "nothing" even though there was something. I could tell.

Then one evening I found out. I think I was at cheerleading practice when my dad told my mom what was going on. He was having an affair. When my mom told me what he had said I was so mad. I thought I was going to spit fire. Evidently, my dad was having an affair for some time and his feelings had changed for my mom. I blamed myself for the longest time. I thought it was my fault for keeping them apart for so long while I had to see if I could reach the Olympics or at least get a scholarship to make them proud. And that thought still hangs in the back of my mind to this day even though my parents preach that it's not my fault. It's not a thought that I can just turn off. Like feelings for someone; you can't just turn them off. If I could start over, I'd trade my gymnastics for my parents' marriage in a second. But I can't.

Children pay a heavy emotional price when their parents divorce. Relatives are also pushed into awkward and difficult situations in relating to the divorced parties.

Because of the painful consequences, you have natural constraints for staying married. While natural constraints may not keep you married, your spiritual commitment may deepen your resolve to continue to work on your marriage. Peter wrote, "In the same way, you wives must accept the authority of your husbands, even those who refuse to accept the Good News. Your godly lives will speak to them better than any words. They will be won over by watching your pure, godly behavior."[5]

3. *Accept, don't expect.* There has to be an awareness that there is no one or anything that will ever disappoint you. When your husband lets you down, then he has failed to meet one of your expectations of him. Knowing that was like

a light going on for a couple I (Gary) counseled. I said, "You cannot have unrealistic expectations of one another." Her expectations of her husband had driven him away from her.

What is the difference between a valid expectation and an unrealistic one? A valid expectation is based on a realistic commitment mutually agreed upon by you and your partner. An unrealistic expectation may be something you have unilaterally decided based on your upbringing or role models (or lack of them) for husbands. Surrender your unrealistic expectations. Lay them at the foot of the cross and refuse to pick them up again.

You may dream and have goals. Surrendering unrealistic expectations doesn't mean that you wander aimlessly, but if you have your own personal expectations of him, you are setting yourself up for disappointment every step of the way. Unfulfilled expectations create anger. You can expect certain actions or attitudes of yourself but not of him.

Acceptance is another matter. Scripture clearly commands, "Accept one another, then, just as Christ accepted you, in order to bring praise to God."[6]

Acceptance invites your husband to move toward you while unrealistic expectations drive him away. Let me give you an example. You may expect your husband to call you if he is going to be five minutes late in picking you up. It's important to move beyond the level of being legalistic. Legalistic expectations create a lack of trust between you and your husband.

Decide to accept him and to pull with him instead of against him. At times, he will be the stronger partner in your marriage and will be helping you through difficult circumstances. At other times, you will be the stronger one.

4. *Focus on solutions, not problems.* It's so important to focus on the present and building your foundation for the future. Old materials from the past cannot build a new, safe home for the future. Don't dig up all the past mistakes that a present stumble may prompt you to remember. Choose to forgive the past so that you will not drag it into your present rebuilding process.

No digging permitted. Imagine remodeling a room and choosing to use an old, rotten beam that you have just removed as the support for a new ceiling, wall, or floor. What a foolish thing it would be to do new construction with old, damaged materials. Likewise, refuse to bring up old hurts and pain as you develop your plan for winning your husband back. The key is to focus on the present and on potential solutions. For example, if adultery has affected your marriage, going back to all the graphic details will not help to heal your relationship. Forgive and bury the past. Focusing on the past and specific problems keeps you from seeing the future and the solutions to the problem. Set a boundary and establish a rule: No digging permitted!

Remember what worked, not what didn't work. Some wonderful attitudes and behaviors attracted your husband to you earlier in your marriage. Furthermore, there have probably been times in your relationship that were good. The question to ask yourself is, What was different about those times? What was I doing different? What were we doing differently? Notice that we didn't suggest you ask, "What was my husband doing differently?" The reason is it's probably easy to remember what he was doing wrong. But again, we want the focus to remain on what you can do. Get beyond the rotten wood to the framework and foundation that gave life and spark to your marriage.

Affirm in yourself and your husband the qualities that enhance your marriage instead of focusing on the problems and defects. You want to find the exceptions to your problems. We want you to become proactive in looking for things that used to cause relational satisfaction. Become solution-focused instead of problem-focused.

We have a wonderful African violet story that fits well at this point. Milton Erickson, a now-deceased psychiatrist, has related the story of how he once went to the home of a friend in Milwaukee. His friend had a Christian aunt there who was very old and very wealthy. She lived in a huge Victorian home with incredible antiques, but his friend was concerned because she was depressed. And so Milton went to the home at his friend's request to visit this aunt.

The aunt took him on a tour of her entire home. All the blinds were closed. It was dark, gloomy, and depressing. The last room she took him into was her African violet room where she grew gorgeous African violets. So as Milton the psychiatrist went back out to the patio, he said to her, "I can see what your problem is."

She said, "What do you mean?"

He said, "You are not really a very good Christian."

"What do you mean?" she asked, rather insulted.

He said, "Well, here you have this great gift for growing African violets, and you keep it all to yourself." He said, "If I were you, I would go to your church and get your bulletin, and whenever someone had a birthday, or a death, or a wedding, or an anniversary, or whatever, I would take them a gift of African violets."

As Erickson told me the story of this woman, he pulled out an old, yellowed newspaper from Milwaukee. A front-page headline read, "African Violet Queen of Milwaukee Dies . . . Mourned by Thousands."

That aunt of Erickson's friend took to heart what he said to her. After he left, she started doing exactly as he said. She began growing violets throughout her home. More windows were opened and light filled the previously dark house. As her violets bloomed she took them to people all over Milwaukee. She made friends and invited them over to see her violets. All of this led to her developing an incredible life of ministering to others.

Erickson was asked by the nephew, "What made you think of that rather than treating her for depression?"

He said, "I decided that it would be easier to grow the African violet part of her life than to weed out the depression."

That is a great picture for winning your husband back. Instead of focusing on trying to weed out the problems in your relationship, turn your attention to what solutions are needed to enhance your relationship. For example, you might be thinking, *It would help our relationship if my husband would stop making me feel like everything else is a priority. His job, friends, and leisure activities all make me feel like I am number seven or eight on his priority list.* How many of us have felt like that before? The problem is, the focus is still on what's not working, or as Dr. Erickson explained, on weeding out the depression. If your goal is to feel like a priority, look for times that your husband does make you feel like a priority. It could be any seemingly insignificant little thing he does. Solution-focused thinking would be, "When you picked up your cereal bowl and put it in the dishwasher, that made me feel like a priority. It made me feel like you were recognizing how important it is for me to have you help out around the house." Then you could go on: "If you really wanted to blow me away, you would also do _____. Thank you for making me feel like a priority." Notice that by focusing on the positives—the exceptions, it keeps the conversation in the realm of solutions.

Keeping your eyes focused on what works, instead of the problems, is vital for growing the African violets in your life. You may feel discouraged because your husband does not prize your gifts and this has shut out the sunlight so your violets have not grown. Discover what your violets are and let them grow. Give these gifts of beauty to him in the relationship. Examples of his African violets would be affirmation of his strengths, encouragement of his gifts, and honoring his accomplishments.

If your husband has become disinterested in you, you may need to develop your own African violets. Begin opening up some rooms in the house that you're renovating to let the light in so that they will be attractive to him. You cannot give what you are not growing in yourself.

A potential trap in winning your husband back is trying to become what you think he expects you to be. The key to your plan is asking this: "Lord, who have You called me to be?"

One of the toughest things you may need to do in winning your husband back is to begin honoring him. Because of the hurt and pain in your strained relationship now, honoring your husband will take a strong commitment. We can now turn to this important next step.

Chapter Six

Honor Your Husband

God has built into every man the natural ability to be the very loving leader his family needs.

—Gary Smalley[1]

I recently moved out of our family home to be on my own with my two daughters from previous marriages. My husband, Kevin, and I agreed that the move would be only a trial separation to help "clear the air." However, a short time later Kevin came to my apartment to talk. "I'm filing for divorce," he said matter-of-factly. "You should move on with your life." I sat there for the longest time not knowing how to respond. "Is this what you mean by 'clearing the air'?" I yelled in a sarcastic voice as Kevin moved toward the door. "I still love you and probably always will." And then he was gone.

Approximately one month later I received my divorce papers. And then the bomb hit. Someone told me that he was seeing another woman. To make circumstances even harder, the woman was also going through a divorce and attended the church where my family and I worshiped.

Over the following weeks, I walked into church with my head held high. It was the grace of God that allowed me to stand in view of everyone and still receive the comfort I so desperately needed from God. The relationship between my husband and his new "friend" became increasingly bolder and they were finally asked to choose between doing what was right—God's Word—and their own way. They have now left the church, along with all the members of her family and their immediate friends.

I do not want to end my marriage. I believe with all my heart that God would not break up two marriages to bring two people together. I have prayed diligently for reconciliation with my husband. I pray daily for the Lord to have His way in my marriage.

In all your examples, Gary, you advise women to show interest, adoration, genuine love, respect, submission, and honor to their husbands. But how can I when Kevin will not even talk to me? I have discussed the situation with my pastor. He advises that I should consecrate my husband to the Lord and let Him work out the situation.

Our Highest Calling: Honor

This precious wife has asked one of the most important questions we know of: How do I honor my husband in spite of what he does? Attempting to answer this question begins with an understanding that genuine love is a gift we give. It isn't purchased by actions or contingent upon our emotions. It may carry strong emotional feelings, but it isn't supported by them. Rather, to love is a decision we make daily toward someone who is special and valuable to us. As with genuine love, honor is a gift we give to someone. Honoring involves making the decision to highly value someone even before we put love into action. In many cases, love often begins to flow once we have made the decision to honor that person.

How do we make love a decision? This question was answered many years ago when Jesus spoke to a young lawyer, "Love the Lord your God with all your heart and with all your soul and with all your mind . . . [and] love your neighbor as yourself."[2] This verse illustrates three of the highest and most revered aspects of love: loving God, loving others, and finding value in ourselves.

This verse is also the essence of honor. Marital expert Dr. John Gottman has discovered through his research essentially what the Scriptures have been stating for centuries: The absolute key to a healthy relationship is honor. It is the greatest of all commandments.[3]

There are countless definitions of the word *honor*. We define *honor* as "a decision expressed by placing high value, worth, and importance on another person, viewing that person as a priceless gift, and respectfully granting him or her a place in one's life."

To further clarify honor before we apply it, let's look at what it is not. As we wrote in *Bound by Honor,* "*Dishonor* is something or someone who has little worth, weight, or value." When we dishonor people, we consciously or unknowingly treat them as having little importance or value. Anger, sarcasm, unjust criticism, unhealthy comparisons, favoritism, inconsistency, jealousy, selfishness, envy, racism, and a host of other ills are "justified" as legal weapons to use against people we consider of little value. The lower the value we attach to people, the easier we can "justify" dishonoring them with our words or treating them with disrespect.

Dishonor roots itself in a self-righteous and arrogant attitude. When we dishonor a spouse, we treat him in an inferior way while we assume a superior attitude. Honor mirrors the kind of humility that Jesus exemplified:

> Is there any encouragement from belonging to Christ? Any comfort from his love? Any fellowship together in the Spirit? Are your hearts tender and sympathetic? Then make me truly happy by agreeing wholeheartedly with each other, loving one another, and working together with one heart and purpose. Don't be selfish; don't live to make a good impression on others.
>
> Be humble, thinking of others as better than yourself. Don't think only about your own affairs, but be interested in others, too, and what they are doing. Your attitude should be the same that Christ Jesus had. Though he was God, he did not demand and cling to his rights as God. He made himself nothing; he took the humble position of a slave and appeared in human form. And in human form he obediently humbled himself even further by dying a criminal's death on a cross.[4]

Jesus' attitude was that of a servant. When both you and your husband have a servant attitude toward each other, then you will be honoring each other.

If we're serious about honoring God, our mate, our children, and others, we'll begin to combat our natural bent to dishonor them by taking them lightly. How can we do that? We can begin by understanding two aspects of the definition of honor.

1. *A priceless treasure.* "Where your treasure is, there your heart will be also."[5] As this verse explains, you show honor to God and your husband by viewing them as costly gifts or special treasures. For instance, you can see your husband as the world's largest diamond. Let's be honest. Sometimes the decision to treat a mate as a costly gift has to be made on an hourly basis! When we view someone as a priceless diamond then our positive feelings for them increase. What a rich dividend.

2. *A highly respected position.* Not only does honor apply to someone we consider a priceless treasure, it can be used for someone who occupies a highly respected position, someone high on our priority list. What if you do not "feel" like granting a person respect? The good news is that positive feelings usually follow the decision to honor someone. What place does your husband feel he has in your life? If you want honor to shine brightly at home then you will make sure your husband feels like a number one priority.

In our lives we have times in which we have no motivation to do important tasks, but we do them anyway. We need to administer medicine to our two-year-old even when she refuses to take it. Or we may have to stay up late to finish the report by its deadline—no matter how it bends our schedule or robs us of sleep. Or perhaps we need to wake up an hour earlier than normal each day to exercise and spend time in the Word and in prayer. Whatever the situation, we have times when all our natural instincts may say no, but God's Word, or another person's best interest, demands we say yes.

So how do you apply honor within your marital relationship? The answer might surprise you.

Using Honor to Win Your Husband Back

In winning your husband back, it's important to renovate areas in your relationship that will serve as places you both can enjoy. Imagine decorating a room in a home that everyone can enjoy. It is a cozy place, filled with scented candles and soft light. The window coverings and accessories in the room are pleasing and tasteful. The colors in the room have been carefully selected to reflect the most refined tastes of both you and your husband. This is an inviting room for conversation, closeness, and intimacy. It's a place where you both feel comfortable.

When decorating such a room, you might make a list of all the items needed to make it a beautiful place. The same is true in rebuilding a relationship to win your husband back. It's important to make a list of the God-given things you admire most about your husband and the gifts God has given you as well.

Gifts God Has Given You	Gifts God Has Given Your Husband
_____	_____
_____	_____
_____	_____
_____	_____
_____	_____

When you made your list of all the admirable gifts God gave your husband, you began a process of honoring him.

Honor not only lists the positive, God-given attributes in a spouse, it also practices praising God for them and speaking them often to the other person. What you sow into the life of another person, you will reap. Sow love and reap a harvest of love. Sow honor and esteem and reap the same. Likewise, sow dishonor and a harvest of hurt and pain will grow.

Be careful at this point. You are not honoring what he is not. Truthfully focus on what you can honestly esteem in him and stop criticizing what he is not. Flattery focuses on what is not true or only superficial. Honor encourages what is true.

These lists are not intended to flatter you or your husband. In fact, you may not even have the opportunity to share this list even for a few months. The lists are primarily for your sake, not his. They will benefit your feelings and emotions about God, yourself, and your husband. Seek to cultivate these gifts daily in yourself and in him.

God has given you both awesome gifts to share in your marriage. It's time that you reach out to Him together for His help in using those gifts.

Your husband may now seem very closed to you, but you are now ready to take some steps toward opening his closed spirit. Believe it or not, it's still possible for him to open up to you!

Chapter . . . .
Seven . . . .

Open Your Husband's Closed Spirit

In your anger do not sin: Do not let the sun go down while
you are still angry, and do not give the devil a foothold.
—Ephesians 4:26–27 NIV

We've observed that anger has many tragic consequences in a marriage or family. Let's look at three of
the most deadly results.

1. *Anger creates distance.* If you are married to an angry person, he or she will usually try to create distance between you.
You may want to get close, but the offended one will pull
away. Angry people refuse closeness. Improve the relationship, and they'll sabotage it. Call it black, and they'll call it
white—just to keep you at arm's length. In most cases, however, distance is a destroyer. It causes husbands and wives,
parents and children to drift away from one another. Home
becomes little more than a dormitory with hostile roommates.

2. *Anger pushes us into darkness.* The apostle John sketched
a striking true-life portrait of what happens to those who

cling to anger: "Anyone who claims to be in the light but hates his brother is still in the darkness. Whoever loves his brother lives in the light, and there is nothing in him to make him stumble. But whoever hates his brother is in the darkness and walks around in the darkness; he does not know where he is going, because the darkness has blinded him."[1]

Unresolved anger does that in our lives. It rips away our perspective and throws us into chaos. We don't know where we are. We can't think logically. We don't realize what we're doing to ourselves and those we love. Further, walking consistently in darkness prevents us from being sensitive or loving toward others. It also kills any interest we have in studying God's Word and lays any desire to pray in the deep-freeze. Anger also robs us of any desire to please and honor God or to experience His joy, contentment, and peace.

3. *Anger ties us in knots.* Like few other emotions, anger restricts and binds us, tying us in internal knots. Like rope tied around our feet or hands, anger hinders and hampers us. Our mate and children who reside in an angry and embittered home become handcuffed and hobbled. Further, they are prevented from discovering their potential. But seeking their forgiveness is like releasing them from tight ropes that grip their lives and cut off life-giving circulation. The following story illustrates the power of opening your husband's closed spirit.

When I (Mary) was young, I was told I was a beautiful girl and very sweet. I would lie awake in bed dreaming that surely somebody would love me unconditionally, and save me from the horrible nightmare of physical and sexual abuse. But no one came.

I eventually met Bart, my husband. He was my knight in

shining armor, different from the rest. So I married him, still not knowing what true love was. He comes from a loving, God-fearing family. His was a family that rejected me from the start. For four years, I worshiped the ground my husband walked on. I tried unsuccessfully to gain the attention and respect I deserved from my in-laws. They had very little to do with us, even when their first and only grandson was born. I was rejected again. I was getting frustrated and angry! Why would no one pay me any attention? I just wasn't good enough for anyone.

Then the affairs started. In a period of eight years, I had six different affairs. It was an extremely confusing time for me. Our marriage was not a bad one, where we fought or where any kind of abuse was present, but it certainly wasn't a God-centered marriage. Shortly after we were married I confessed to Bart about my past—but not the affairs. There were abortions, a sexually transmitted disease, a previous husband and two children. But, praise God, Bart loved me and still does today. That required godly strength, nothing else could come close.

Over the next several months, the Holy Spirit worked in my life. I became convicted that I needed to confess the affairs to my husband. I realized that until I could be totally honest, we would not be able to have the type of satisfying relationship that I longed for.

Here is Bart's account of that night:

While sitting on our bed, I balled up both my fists as if in anger, and told the woman I love so much that I've got so much anger inside myself and it's got to come out. But before we start I want us to agree that we both love each other, we are adults, and that everyone makes mistakes. We can't go back and change what happened "yesterday." But most of all I want you to know I love you. I'm not going to get mad or angry, I'm not going to hurt you. We need to agree that we will go back to the day we met, and we will discuss everything. But most of all, we agree to be truthful and honest about everything, and nothing will be held back.

To this my loving wife responded, "Okay." So I began with small unimportant questions, which led to when I first suspected her involvement with another man. Her response was, "I'm not ready to talk about this." However, after a few minutes of talking I asked the same question again, to which she replied, "Yes, I had been involved with this man for a period of time."

From that point, I chronologically walked through five affairs. I know now in my heart that this was God's way of showing me that my wife was being totally honest with me. This in turn, brought about comfort and security, to know that I could finally trust and believe her.

Soon we were both exhausted. We tried to sleep, but in the early morning hours I was awakened by the most frightening thing I've ever known. I was weeping out of control. I said some things to my wife including, "I want a divorce."

She slid across the bed, put her arms around me, and said, "I'm sorry. Can you please forgive me?" It was like every bit of the hurt left me instantly. The love returned and has been there without question ever since.

Mary: So now we are starting over and it's better than it has ever been for one reason: God is at the center of the relationship.

Bart and Mary are true examples of the healing power of dissolving anger and bitterness in our mate's heart. As we wrote in *The Key to Your Child's Heart*, after witnessing first-hand the devastation that anger can produce in a family or relationship, we have identified five crucial attitudes that can drain even long-held anger from a person's heart and life:

1. *Become soft and tender with the person.* The first step is to become soft in your mind and spirit. Lower your voice and relax your facial expressions. This reflects honor and humility; and as Proverbs 15:1 suggests, "A gentle answer turns away [anger]."

2. *Understand, as much as possible, what your husband has endured.* It's important to genuinely understand the pain your husband feels and how he has interpreted your offensive behavior. Ask for his interpretation of what occurred. The goal is to listen and understand what your mate is feeling. Resist defending yourself, lecturing, or questioning why he did or didn't do something. The best way to accomplish this is by using the "Drive-through Listening" technique described on pages 128–31.

3. *Admit your husband has been wounded and admit any wrong in provoking that hurt.* The third step is to take ownership of your offensive behavior. A husband feels valuable when he hears you admit your mistake and sees that you understand how he feels. Sometimes this is all it takes to open a closed spirit.

4. *Touch him gently.* If you try to touch someone with a spirit knotted in anger, you will find out just how deep the hurt is. The first response may very well be a stiffening or pulling away—but persistent softness expressed in meaningful

touches, like the gentle massage of a knotted muscle, can go a long way toward draining anger and negative feelings.

5. *Seek forgiveness—and wait for a response.* The final step is to give your husband the opportunity to respond to your confession. Just as Mary demonstrated, ask if he could find it in his heart to forgive you. You'll know true restoration has occurred when forgiveness is granted and he allows you to touch him.

Anger restricts and binds us, tying us in internal knots. Forgiveness, on the other hand, sets us free from those bonds, untying the knots that hold us captive. The Lord Jesus gives us a powerful word picture of forgiveness in Luke 6:37, when He says, "Forgive, and you will be forgiven." The word He uses for *forgive* in the original language literally means "to release fully, to unbind or to let go." It is the only time in the New Testament that this word is translated "forgive." In every other instance, it means "release" or "free," as when Lazarus exited the tomb, bound hand and foot in grave clothes, and Jesus said, "Unbind him, and let him go."

What If Your Husband Refuses to Forgive?

If you have followed these five steps and your husband refuses to forgive you, there are several possible reasons. Perhaps the offense was deeper than you realized or he wants to see your behavior change first. Whatever the reason, the best thing is to be patient. No matter how he responds, never drop the issue altogether simply because he isn't ready to forgive you. Let the situation cool off for a while, then come back and repeat the five steps.

For many people, men in particular, sharp words can set off a defensive reaction, even another round of battle. But men or women who are wise enough to untie the anger knot in another's heart will learn to listen beyond the sharp words, to the hurt feelings behind the emotional outburst. Tension is in some of those knots. Untying them may release some of the negative feelings held in check. Your focus should be on untying the knots and releasing the anger even when it becomes uncomfortable for you.

As angry as you may be with your husband, can you forgive? Your next step—to forgive—will require great courage.

Chapter ....
Eight ....

Forgive

A Christian will find it cheaper to pardon than to resent. Forgiveness saves the expense of anger, the cost of hatred, the waste of spirits.

—Hannah More

The happiest people are less forgetting and more forgiving.

—Anonymous

"Daddy Threw My Popcorn Away!"

"Is it time for our special date?" begged Taylor early Saturday morning. Blinking hard, I (Greg) tried to focus on who'd summoned me out of deep sleep. "What time is it?" I said in a groggy voice. "Six-thirty A.M.!" I cried out. But I was just as excited as Taylor. We had been planning this day for the past several weeks. Mommy was going shopping with a friend, so Taylor and I would have the entire day together.

The first part of the day we spent playing around the

house. Then we set out for our favorite eating spot . . . Chuck E. Cheese! We stuffed ourselves with pizza and played for hours. We were both feeling close to each other. I smiled proudly when she rushed over, threw her arms around me, and yelled, "Daddy . . . I love you so much."

The next part of our special date took us to the movie theater. Taylor had been talking nonstop about some *George of the Jungle* movie. She'd seen the commercial and felt her life depended on seeing it. Taylor and I loaded up with popcorn, candy, soda, and some kind of fruity-slushy drink. As my daughter carried her gallon bucket of popcorn and drink down the long hallway, once again she expressed, "Daddy . . . I love you." I was in heaven.

Unfortunately, I had no idea that I was walking into purgatory!

The moment my precious girl sat down in the crowded movie theater, she came to the conclusion that she no longer wanted to see *George of the Jungle*. All she wanted was to be someplace else. Her only problem, however, was Dad. I'd paid good money to see this movie and for some reason I chose this moment to teach my three-year-old about financial responsibility. The lesson lasted for about .07 seconds, or as long as it takes a three-year-old to scream at such a high pitch that the hair on every neck in the room stood straight up. As people from the back climbed onto their chairs to see what horrible thing was happening, I escorted Taylor out. And despite all my years of psychological training in behavioral modification, I was unable to convince her to watch the movie. Therefore, I did something that I hadn't learned in my doctoral program. I grabbed her bucket of popcorn, stuffed it into the trash, and told her she was in massive trouble. As we stormed down the same long hallway that had once been the site of such nostalgia, her only words now were: "I don't like you!"

When we got home I marched Taylor into her room, told her to go to bed, and slammed the door. Sitting in my chair I tried to determine how our perfect day had become so awful. I soon realized that my frustration seemed more about my expectations than her actions. It was only a $6 movie and we'd had such a good day. Did I really need to react that way? I thought about all the times I'd preached to Taylor, "It's okay to make a mistake, but you need to make it right." I needed to make it right.

I sat on my daughter's bed and held her tight. As her little body shook from all the tears, I told her that Daddy had been wrong to yell and to throw her popcorn away. It was then that she looked up at me and said in the most precious voice, "Daddy, it's okay to make mistakes—you just need to make it up!" Close . . . but at least I knew that she'd been listening.

Seek Forgiveness for Your Wrongdoings

A part of correcting a mistake and making it right is to seek forgiveness. When I (Greg) closed Taylor's spirit by throwing away her popcorn, in order to restore the relationship I needed to make it right by acknowledging my mistake. Likewise, an important first step in winning back your husband is to seek forgiveness for things that you might have done to offend him. Reviewing the last chapter, the steps toward seeking forgiveness are as follows:

• Become soft and tender with your husband.

- Understand, as much as possible, what your husband has endured.
- Admit your husband has been wounded and admit any wrong in provoking that hurt.
- Touch him gently.
- Seek forgiveness—and wait for a response.

The final step is to give your husband the chance to respond to your confession. Ask if he could find it in his heart to forgive you. You'll know true restoration has occurred when forgiveness is granted and he allows you to touch him.

Forgive Your Husband for His Wrongdoings

When we are offended by someone, it can grow into resentment. Resentment in turn can cause anger, bitterness, and unforgiveness to grow like a cancer in your marriage. Left untreated, mildew in a house can grow and begin to cause decay and rot within a home. If not removed, the home may be beautifully renovated but then ruined by the mildew growing inside. So it is with unresolved anger, resentment, and unforgiveness. Jesus is very clear in teaching us about unforgiveness. He said, "If you forgive those who sin against you, your heavenly Father will forgive you. But if you refuse to forgive others, your Father will not forgive your sins."[1] Resentment is automatic distancing in a relationship.

But why is forgiveness important? My youngest son, Michael, who is also a marriage and family therapist, has done extensive study in the area of forgiveness. He has taught us three major reasons why forgiveness is important to your relationship with your husband. The first reason is that we are made in God's image. Being made in God's image carries with it a tremendous amount of honor and responsibility. Honor in knowing our innate value because of our likeness to the Creator. Responsibility because it is God's nature to forgive.

First John 1:9 reads, "If we confess our sins, he is faithful and just and will forgive us our sins and purify us from all unrighteousness." If we are to strive to be more Christlike in everything we do, then forgiveness is incredibly important. If God's nature did not consist of forgiveness, where would we be? God knows the awesome power of forgiveness, and God graciously uses it to cleanse us of all our sins.

The second reason why forgiveness is important lies in the domain of love. Forgiveness is one of the only ways we can love as God loves. When we decide to forgive someone for wrongfully harming us, we are deciding to love them unconditionally. The French writer and moralist, Francois, duc de La Rochefoucauld, wrote in the 1600s: "We pardon to the extent that we love." If we choose not to forgive, then we are putting up limits and boundaries to our love for other people.

Third, forgiveness is freeing to the soul. Forgiveness allows us to break the bonds of anger, rage, hatred, and vengeance. These all lead down the path of destruction. They are like toxins to the soul, and forgiveness is the cleanser. Much of the work in therapy often focuses around the issue of forgiveness. Anger, rage, hatred, and vengeance prevent us from growing to become the mature adults God intended us to be.

But forgiveness is important. If we refuse to forgive others for their mistakes, we are deciding to build a wall in the relationship. Unresolved anger will destroy the relationship with your husband. Even more devastating is the fact that it will hinder your husband's future relationships, especially his relationship with God.

Barriers to Forgiveness

"Why can't I forgive?" is a question on many people's minds. "I know that God wants me to, but I just can't find the strength to go through with it."

Forgiveness is not an easy task. Again, Michael provides three main roadblocks to forgiveness. The first is a lack of responsibility when it comes to owning up to our fallenness. If we are unable to see our own faults and mistakes, how can we possibly move toward forgiveness with our husbands? We must first be able to admit that we are not perfect and that we are capable of hurting our mate.

Second, unresolved anger is a major hindrance to the healing power of forgiveness. If we refuse to let go of bitterness, rage, or hatred we are holding on to very destructive forces. These forces are in direct contrast to the power of forgiveness. The two forces cannot exist together. They are too much a dichotomy for there to be harmony between them.

Finally, many people have great misconceptions about what forgiveness is and therefore struggle with forgiveness because they're on the wrong path. Delusions about forgiveness are dangerous because they are not the truth. The truth will always set us free, like forgiveness. But if we believe the lies about forgiveness then it is natural that we would avoid it at all costs, especially in the light of real emotional pain. One powerful misconception is that we are to "Forgive and forget!" This can be next to impossible. Luckily our brains are not wired to completely forget painful events in our past. Some people might think this was a cruel joke created by God, just to torment us for our sins. But amazingly it is God's blessing that allows us to remember saddening and hurtful experiences from our past. Kin Hubbard once wrote, "Nobody ever forgets where he buried a hatchet."

Sandi illustrated this misconception through her letter:

I went to a Women of Faith Conference in September. On the way home from the Friday night session one of the gals I was riding with told us that she had heard a definition of forgiveness. She said that true forgiveness is when you give up the right to hurt someone for hurting you. When she said that I thought, *I guess I haven't forgiven my husband because I don't think I've given up my right to hurt him for hurting me.* But then several days later, while reading a devotional, I came to the realization, *No, I have forgiven him.* The devotional stated that forgiveness doesn't mean we stop hurting. Forgiveness doesn't mean these things never happened. I thought, *I have forgiven him. I have forgiven as he did everything.* I told my mom that and she said she thought I had as well. She said if I hadn't forgiven him I couldn't be as kind to him as I was. And I have always been very kind to him throughout our separation.

If we believe we can stuff away our hurts, we are only prolonging the inevitable. By stuffing our hurts deep down in our inner self we are simply waiting for the explosion to occur; like a volcano the intense heat and pressure from past hurts build up, hoping for release, until they finally erupt. Watch out, these eruptions are extremely damaging to family and friends. The ashes or lava will cover everything in its path. Trials and painful experiences are events that God can use in the maturation process of His people! Why would we want to forget? William Meninger wrote:

> Forgiveness, then, is not forgetting. It is not condoning or absolving. Neither is it pretending nor something done for the sake of the offender. It is not a thing we just do by a brutal act of the will. It does not entail a loss of identity, of specialness, or of face. It does not release the offenders from obligations they may or may not recognize. An understanding of these things will go a long way towards helping people enter into the forgiveness process.

Discovering Treasures Within Our Pain

If God's desire is for us not to forget our pain or the trials we experience, how do we reap the benefits of a painful event such as a marital separation, divorce, or an affair? We do this by "treasure-hunting."

> My life is but a weaving, between my God and me,
> I do not choose the colors, he worketh steadily,
> Oftimes He weaveth sorrow, and I in foolish pride,
> Forget He sees the upper, and I the underside.
> Not till the loom is silent, and shuttles cease to fly,
> Will God unroll the canvas and explain the reason why.
> The dark threads are as needful in the skillful Weaver's hand,
> As the threads of gold and silver in the pattern He has planned.

This anonymous poem beautifully illustrates one of the greatest things we can ever learn: the ability to find the "hidden treasure" buried within each difficult experience. The Scriptures assure us that trials and difficult times are unavoidable. Although we may work overtime trying to protect ourselves from pain, we'll never be able to isolate ourselves totally from being hurt by our own or by others' actions. Therefore, we need to teach ourselves how to make "lemonade out of life's lemons." In other words, learning to take any negative experience and actively reverse the damage by turning it into something that we benefit from—like freshly squeezed, sweet lemonade.

When trials crash into our lives, we are instructed to rejoice, knowing that trials bring about many wonderful things. However, don't jump into "treasure-hunting" too fast. When we do not grieve first, it's like looking for buried treasure without a map. We can't go out into our front yard and dig hole after hole unless we have some idea where to start. Grieving provides us with the necessary time to prepare for finding the treasure.

"Treasure-Hunting" Questions

As we wrote in *Bound by Honor,* the process of finding the buried treasures within our pain begins by answering three important questions.

1. *What do you like about yourself?* This first question is not a narcissistic indulgence, but a healthy exercise in personal value. The goal is for you to acquire an accurate view of your positive qualities. For example, What are your strengths? What types of activities are you good at? What do you bring

to a relationship? If you can't think of several strengths, ask a friend, family member, pastor, coworker, or mentor.

2. *What are the most painful trials you've been through?* Here you list the main trials in your life that have caused you pain ... especially the ones that have lowered your self-esteem or where you have felt shame or guilt. If it is too painful to list them all, then focus on two or three and deal with the others another time.

3. *What were the benefits of each trial?* List the positive aspects of each of these painful encounters in your life. For example, crisis situations tend to make you more loving, sensitive, compassionate, thoughtful, gentle, careful, kind, and patient. Usually, the things you like about yourself (question one) develop as a direct result of trials. Besides your own answers, it would be valuable to ask the same question of loved ones. They can often add a perspective to your suffering that you may have overlooked.

As a part of the forgiveness process, we must learn to search for the treasures buried within each trial. As we are able to do this, it can turn negative experiences into positive ones. However, treasure-hunting is not something we do for just a short time; it's something we can continue until we feel the results of God's blessings. This will help us to continue seeing the benefits long after the trial is over. The best part is that we will have written proof that treasures flow from difficult times.

My wife, Norma, echoed the importance of "treasure-hunting" when she was interviewed about how she won me back: "Another thing that really helped me during the years of relational distance with Gary was to keep a journal. I would write down my hurts and trials. For each hurt and trial, I gave thanks to the Lord. I didn't have to feel that way, but out of obedience, I had to give thanks to Christ for what my husband was doing. Then several years later I learned that if I did not take each hurt and look for a benefit, they remained at a negative level—the trial level, full of darkness and gloom. It gave me hope as I forced myself to search for the good."

Action Points Toward Forgiveness

- Make the decision to forgive your husband for his wrongdoings and the pain he has caused you.
- Turn the process over to Christ and ask Him to provide the necessary strength and wisdom to forgive your husband.
- Ask a group of intercessors or an accountability partner to pray for you and to hold you accountable to forgive.
- Treasure-hunt the pain and hurt so you can find the treasures buried within each trial. Sometimes a symbolic act can assist in this process. I've (Greg) had clients write on balloons every hurt and pain someone has caused them. Then I have them go outside and release them to heaven—where they belong. God wants to bear our pain. He sent His Son to die for our sins.

In winning your husband back, you must establish healthy boundaries in your newly emerging relationship with him. Let's discover what those boundaries need to be.

Chapter Nine

Establish Healthy Boundaries

That long [Canadian] frontier from the Atlantic to the Pacific Ocean, guarded only by neighborly respect and honorable obligations, is an example to every country and a pattern for the future of the world.

—Winston Churchill

In the last chapter we dealt with forgiving your husband for mistakes that he has made. Not only do we need to forgive someone when they wrong us, but sometimes we need to place "boundaries" in our relationships to protect ourselves from emotional, spiritual, or physical abuse. Our desire here is to explain how you can control and reduce the impact of others' attempts to steal your happiness. You'll also see how you can decrease your actions that can rob others of happiness.

Jill had been married almost three years when she wrote to us in search of answers to her marital difficulties. Here is her story.

My husband, Matt, has the capability of being a wonderful man and seems to be really struggling with life right now. We have been in marriage counseling almost two years and things only seem to be getting worse.

This week I opened my own checking account, got a post office box, and will be making arrangements with all my creditors to deal with the problems we now face. My husband knows none of this. Since we have been married, we have never filed federal income tax because I can't get him to put his paperwork together. I was counseled to start looking out for myself because he has gotten us in such a financial mess by not paying bills. We've had our electricity and phone turned off numerous times. All the bills go to his office, including my personal bills that I brought into the marriage. I would give him the money to pay them and he would use it for other things. I found out two weeks ago that we are about six months behind in almost all our bills. He told me things had been paid.

Matt is a very smart man, and he can be very kind and tender. However, this part of him has not existed in several years. He hardly talks to people and when he does, criticism and put-downs are commonplace. He won't become a part of our church because he feels that none of the department heads know what they are doing and he won't submit to that. I am the pianist for our church and take my position seriously because I'm doing it as unto the Lord. About the only fellowship I get is with the Praise and Worship Team. Matt has completely quit talking to me. When we go out together he doesn't want to be around me and will run off with others if we are in a group. People at church have been noticing for a long time that his treatment of me is less than desirable. He's rude whenever he speaks and basically ignores me.

Furthermore, Matt's mother has been living with us for quite some time. She will be leaving as soon as a teaching job is secure. I know that this contributes to some of the problems because she supports him. She is a very negative person and will not leave me alone. Since I didn't have a mother while growing up, she insists I need one and is extremely bossy. I'm trying to remain strong, but it is getting more and more difficult.

My question is: Can this marriage be saved? I wish for it to be so because I know he can be a wonderful man. He was the first year we were married, but for the last two years, it has only continued to get worse. We both believe God called us together and when I got married it was for better or worse. I just really struggle right now because I feel like I'm on an emotional roller coaster. I believe prayer works and when you've stood on something, then stand some more; but I can only do this for so long.

Jill has found herself in a very difficult situation. She recognizes that her husband is struggling with several integrity issues. A larger problem, however, is that some of his struggles are putting Jill at risk. His lack of paying bills is making her vulnerable to authorities. We all know how the IRS feels about getting their money. They certainly do not take the approach of, "You haven't ever filed an income tax return . . . No big deal . . . Just pay it whenever you feel like it . . . tomorrow . . . next year . . . whenever. Have a good day." Yeah, right! She could be looking at federal charges and large fines. Other women deal with issues of physical, mental, or spiritual abuse. It is here where forgiveness can take place, but more important, a boundary may need to be put in place.

What Is an Emotional Boundary?

Have you ever seen one of those gigantic yellow bulldozers? The kind that can demolish the sturdiest fences or the strongest of buildings? I (Gary) tend to be a human bulldozer, and no one is more affected by this weakness than my wife. I've lost count of how many times I have bulldozed over her emotional fence. And also, too often I have allowed others to break through my "fence."

As I (Gary)wrote in *Making Love Last Forever,* part of what I've been learning about myself and my relationships is that every one of us has an imaginary fence (emotional boundary) around us—like a property line—that defines where a person starts and ends. It defines who I am, what I am comfortable with, what my needs are, what is appropriate, what is inappropriate, and what causes me to feel safe. It's the same for all of us. Part of a person's unhappiness can relate back to their inability to establish a clear boundary of where his or her identity ends and another person's begins.

My feelings let me know what type of fences I have. If I'm being loved, I have pleasant feelings. If I'm not experiencing love, I may have unpleasant feelings. We often control our feelings based on the fences we set for ourselves. In other words, other people cannot control our feelings. We cannot say, "You keep me upset!" No, we control our choices. We can set limits on what others say to us and what we allow ourselves to do with the information they give us.

Three Types of Fences

A healthy fence can reduce the harm to you, but also allow you to reach out to others in loving and caring ways. Fences are needed for our own happiness and well-being. But some people build fences around themselves that create unhappiness for them and can attempt to rob us of our happiness. So we need to understand them and rebuild any fences that could lead us to unhappiness. There are three kinds of fences. Two of the three are more unhealthy, the third one leans toward the healthy type. As each one is explained, you will probably see yourself in one of the unhealthy types. In your mind, however, keep pushing yourself toward that healthy fence. That's where all of us need to be if we're going to control our own level of happiness.

1. *The fence with the "No Trespassing" sign.* Imagine a fence with a huge sign hanging from one of its pickets stating "No Trespassing." An important aspect of this fence is that it only has a door handle on the *inside* of its gate. The person with this type of fence would be considered withdrawn or distant. They are the kind of person who is disconnected from life, often going out of his or her way to avoid contact with others. But there is also a side of them that can be dominant and aggressive. This person is in deep pain. They close themselves off from all relationships, usually resulting in addictive behaviors to medicate the pain.

2. *The fence with the "Members Only" sign.* In your mind's eye, envision a fence with a sign hanging from a stake saying, "Members Only." This person feels everyone else has a firm grasp on their doorknob, producing more of a codependent type of behavior toward others. This sort of person brings the

entire family inside his fence. His spouse is there, along with all the kids; but that's usually where it stops. No one else is allowed in and, of course, there is no doorknob on the outside. This person's life is completely wrapped around the lives of others close to him or her . . . usually the family. The problem here is simple: There is no clear sense of personal identity. The fences are shared. His fence is your fence. It's not, "I have a problem." Instead, it's, "We have a problem." Anything that bothers him is something that bothers all around him. They find their identity with whomever they are with.

These first two fences are more unhealthy in nature, while this last fence reflects positive health. Let's take a look.

3. *The fence with the "Welcome" sign.* This fence has a gate with a doorknob on both sides, and a "Welcome" sign hanging out front. This fence promotes sharing and true intimacy. This person knows where he or she ends and another begins. This single concept has been of more help to me in my marriage than any other principle in the last ten years. I'm a changed man in my marriage—changed for the better. For example, I've learned to knock on my wife's gate instead of bulldozing my way in as I did in the past. When I knock, I ask my wife, "May I come in and talk?" And she has the freedom to say, "Yes" or "No." I have learned to accept her answer too. If she says, "No. Let's talk later," I know that is best and wait for the proper time.

Remember, if we want to experience personal happiness, we must take 100 percent control of our lives, including how we respond to others. You can sum this all up in two very significant observations, both of which contribute to our level of happiness in life. I call them the two sides of a healthy gate.

One observation concerns others, the second concerns you. Both of them must be kept in mind to experience personal happiness.

1. You will always have people who want to get inside "your fence" without your permission.
2. We are responsible to build our own fence and lovingly tell people where our property line begins and ends, based on our own needs and feelings.

Jill from the above story learned firsthand that many husbands are masters at getting inside emotional fences. However, Jill is also 100 percent responsible for establishing her emotional property line. As she noted at the beginning of her story, Jill has acted on that responsibility by opening her own checking account, getting a post office box, and planning to make arrangements with her creditors to deal with the problems. She may also need to set additional boundaries with her husband concerning future financial issues and how long her mother-in-law can stay at their house.

Boundary setting can be extremely difficult for some personality types. We teach a personality session at our monthly seminar. We divide individuals into four categories and name these categories according to four animals (Lion, Otter, Beaver, and Golden Retriever). The Golden Retriever type of personality typically has difficulty establishing personal boundaries. These people are usually warm and relational, great listeners, enjoy routine, have sensitive feelings, are peacemakers, extremely loyal, and have great need for security and an agreeable environment. Their greatest challenge is to learn to say no (set boundaries) and to learn to confront others when they are wounded emotionally.

No matter what your personality type or situation, it is very important to gain a realistic understanding of where personal boundaries need to be placed within the relationship with your husband. We encourage you to discuss boundary setting with some friends, intercessors, a counselor, mentors, or an accountability partner. For example, if you are being physically abused in any way, your safety is the primary concern. Before any attempt to win your husband back can be made, he must get professional help in managing his anger. Studies have shown that group intervention programs can be effective in treating domestic abuse perpetrators. Furthermore, if your husband is physically or sexually abusing you or your children then you must get to safety. Call the police, stay with a family member, friend, pastor, coworker, or at a women's shelter— but get your family out of the abusive situation. Other types of boundary issues to consider include:

- Sexual relationship with husband while separated or divorced
- Phone calling
- Letter writing
- Dating other people
- Emotionally abusive conversations
- Financial arrangements for you and the kids
- Personal property
- Living arrangements

Now that you have begun the process of establishing emotional and physical boundaries with your husband, it's time to address the issue of communication. Winning your husband back requires that both you and your husband communicate effectively and positively with one another. If the commitment and dedication are there for you, then it's time to start communicating your feelings and actions.

Chapter
Ten

Communicate!

He who restrains his words has knowledge,
And he who has a cool spirit is a man of understanding.
—Proverbs 17:27 NASB

After living separate lives, a retired business executive and his wife discovered a painful reality. Sitting at home one evening, the couple called some friends to see what they were doing. "Oh," said the other wife, "we're just talking and drinking tea."

The executive's wife hung up the phone. "Why don't we ever do that?" she demanded. "They're just drinking tea and talking."

"So," said the executive, "make us some tea." Soon they sat with their freshly brewed tea, staring at each other. "Call them back," he directed, "and find out what they're talking about!"

As the couple discovered, a relationship will be only as good as its communication.

Whenever Sarah would get angry, she would vent her anger on her husband, Larry. Early in their marriage, Larry would silently listen and rarely give any feedback. However, he began to withdraw emotionally from intimacy in their marital relationship, and he started to work late and find excuses to go out with the guys after work and on weekends. Larry simply couldn't handle all the negative emotions that Sarah would dump on him.

They weren't communicating. Communication is a two-way dialogue with both partners sharing and listening. In Sarah and Larry's marriage, the dialogue had disintegrated into a monologue with Sarah overwhelming Larry with words and emotions. As he withdrew, she became anorexic and bulimic. For six weeks, Sarah fought her eating disorders in a psychiatric hospital. While she was in the hospital, Larry went with some friends to a Promise Keepers rally. There he renewed his commitment to God and his marriage.

Sarah and Larry decided to go to a Christian counselor and work on their marriage relationship. Even though Larry was committed to the marriage, he could no longer tolerate Sarah's dumping all her negative feelings on him. The counselor helped them practice a very important communication skill—listening to one another.

Sarah admitted that she talked too much and never listened to Larry. So, each day they spent thirty minutes together sharing and listening. To start their time together each day, Larry, not Sarah, would talk for fifteen minutes while Sarah listened. She didn't say one word in response to anything he said. Sarah kept herself from responding defensively or negatively. She simply listened. At times, she would sob or even cry angrily. But she continued to listen. Slowly both Sarah and Larry learned how to listen to one another, communicate positively, and rebuild their relationship.

Sarah has also learned how to dump her anger and negative feelings on the cross and not on Larry. She shared, "I can visualize the cross where I unload all my garbage. When I do that within forty-eight hours of a hurtful episode, I become a totally different person for Larry to talk within our marriage." To win your husband back, positive communication is essential!

Communication That Can Cause Further Distance

Return with me to the house we are renovating. Imagine having the entire house renovated without electricity or phone lines. The house might look great but nothing could function inside the house. No appliances or equipment would work. That would render the house virtually uninhabitable. Likewise, you can do everything we have discussed up to this point and still not be moving any closer together as a couple because your communication isn't effective.

Most wives can immediately identify all the things their husbands are doing wrong, but it's more difficult to recognize what they themselves are doing wrong. We often have difficulty recognizing our own shortcomings. Now it's time to identify what you may be doing or saying to cause further distance between you and your husband.

1. *Overwhelming your husband after work with problems.* After dealing with work situations on the job, you can simply overwhelm your husband with domestic and marital problems

when he walks through the door. Dumping all your problems on him will only drive your husband farther away.

If he continually comes home thinking that conflict will engulf him the moment he opens the door, at some point he will start coming home later or not at all. Simply put, men hate walking in the door and immediately having to solve problems. Added to work problems, problems at home simply produce overload. The natural instinct is to fight or to flee. After enough fighting, he will flee the marriage.

2. *Too many words*. You may be talking your marriage to death. When a sentence or phrase might do to communicate, you may be dumping a paragraph or essay. Talking about your problems all the time focuses your and your husband's attention on the negatives in your marriage instead of the positives.

The right words in a marriage can greatly facilitate communication.

- Words that are salty create a thirst in your husband to listen.
- Words that are affirming motivate your husband to listen.
- Words that are accepting invite your husband to share.
- Words that are forgiving release your husband to admit failure.

But the wrong words in a marriage, and too many of them, can block communication and drive a husband away both emotionally and physically.

- Words that blame and accuse cause a husband to become defensive.

- Words that overflow saturate a husband with burdens and heaviness.
- Words that continually analyze or explain force a husband to become a counseling client instead of a mate.
- Words that try to spiritualize your situation project an attitude of spiritual superiority or condemnation.

Be certain that your communication is a dialogue, not a monologue. Try to listen more than you speak. James gave good advice here, "Dear friends, be quick to listen, slow to speak, and slow to get angry. Your anger can never make things right in God's sight."[1]

3. *No rules for fighting.* When both of you need to discuss volatile issues and don't fight fair, then barriers are erected blocking communication between the two of you. If there is conflict but no rules in your relationship, then the reasons for your conflict may be:

- One of you is trying to exercise power and control in the relationship.
- One of you feels insecure.
- The two of you have differences in values.
- You compete with one another.
- Personal differences exist in the relationship.
- There are misunderstood feelings and unmet needs in your marriage.

When you are attacking your husband without respect for his feelings, you are fighting without rules. Conflicts can become a door to intimacy if we value one another more than winning. The basic rule of conflict needs to be "Everybody wins." This rule means that both you and your husband keep working on a solution to the conflict until both of you feel good about the resolution.

Check off the "Fighting Rules" that you do not keep and you need to start abiding by:

___ Clarify what the actual conflict is.

___ Stick to the issue at hand.

___ Maintain as much tender physical contact as possible, like holding hands.

___ Avoid sarcasm.

___ Avoid "you" statements.

___ Don't use "hysterical statements" that exaggerate or overgeneralize.

___ Resolve any hurt feelings before continuing the conflict discussion.

___ Don't use name-calling.

___ Avoid power actions or statements like "I quit" or "You're killing me."

___ Don't use the silent treatment.

___ Keep your arguments as private as possible.

___ Repeat back or paraphrase what you think the other person is saying.

___ Resolve your conflicts with a win-win solution.

___ Strive to reflect honor and respect for your mate.

4. *Projecting blame.* It's important for you to take responsibility for your own feelings, actions, and words. Another basic rule in conflict resolution is to speak for yourself and take responsibility for your feelings, attitudes, and actions. Refuse to project blame by making statements such as

"You make me feel . . ." or "You are wrong to say or do . . ." These statements shut the door on communication. Other door-slammers are sarcasm, denial, and disrespect. Door-openers for both partners are kindness, respect, and calmness.

5. *Using harsh communication.* This happens when we use labels or resort to name-calling in a relationship. Put-downs immediately distance husband and wives from one another. Using profanity or cursing also pushes our mates away.

Indirect harsh communication is very damaging to your marital relationship as well. When you speak harshly about your mate to family, relatives, or friends, you increase the likelihood that someone else will become angry with your mate. The more people involved with your angry feelings, the more distance you will create, not only among you and your husband but also between others and him. If you cannot speak positively about your mate to others, then maintain gracious silence.

A. W. Tozer in his *Five Vows for Spiritual Power* urges that we vow "never to pass anything on about anyone else that would hurt him."[2] Long after you have forgiven your mate for something he did to hurt you, your harsh communication to others about him may continue to produce bitterness in them and become a constant reminder to you of past pain.

Ways to Communicate Effectively

You can keep your communication at an effective level of communication through LUVR: Listen, Understand, Validate, and Respond. Plan to do this unilaterally since your husband may not yet be open to positive communication.

You are establishing the flow of communication and the rules for fighting.

- *Listen.* By listening to him you communicate that he is a person of worth and what he says is important.
- *Understand.* You may have to paraphrase back to him what you hear him saying so that you clearly understand what he has said: "What I just heard you say was . . ."
- *Validate.* Then he can verify or correct until he is saying and you are hearing exactly what he means. You can affirm him by understanding what is communicated and validating the communication.
- *Respond.* At this point, you can decide how to respond to what your husband has said.

Communication is not a war where one spouse tries to overcome or barrage the other until one wins and the other loses. Communication is mutual understanding and affirmation.

Also remember that much of communication is nonverbal. It's not what you say but how you say it: facial expressions, tone of voice, and body language. The end result of communication has to be win-win in which both of you feel understood and accepted even if there is disagreement over differing opinions.

If you have difficulty communicating with each other, you may need to try ways other than face-to-face communication.

Drive-through listening helps you stay focused and targeted in your communication. It's a quick back-and-forth method much like the drive-through at a fast-food place. Picture yourself ordering at a McDonald's drive-through window. As you look over the menu, a voice from the speaker box says, "May I take your order?"

"I'll have a cheeseburger, fries, and a large Coke," you confidently say.

After a short moment of silence, the voice repeats, "You want a burger, fries, and a large Diet Coke?"

"NO!" you shout in the direction of the speaker box. "A *cheese*burger, fries, and a large *Coke*!"

"Sorry," the box responds, "You want a cheeseburger, fries, and a large Coke. Will that be all?"

"Yes," you confirm.

"That will be $2.99. Have a nice day."

This is a good example of effective communication that should take place in marriage. When you want your mate to clearly and accurately understand your "order," you should use the "drive-through listening" method. One of you becomes the customer and the other becomes the employee. As the customer, you first explain your feelings or needs by using "I feel" statements—as opposed to "You make me feel" remarks. "I feel" messages enable you to take 100 percent responsibility for your feelings and statements. It's also helpful to use short sentences so your husband can repeat back precisely what you are communicating.

Next, your mate simply repeats what he heard. Then you get to "edit" his interpretation. After correcting any misunderstandings, your husband continues to repeat your statements back until you feel your feelings and needs are understood.

Once you are finished sharing, trade places. Your husband becomes the customer and you get to be the employee. He then places his order by explaining his feelings and needs.

Your job is to repeat back what you hear him communicating until he is satisfied. This sequence continues until everyone feels heard and understood. The beauty of this method is that it allows LUVR to take place—Listening, Understanding, Validating, and Responding. Here is why. In order to accurately repeat what you are hearing someone say, you have to listen closely. Listening and repeating lead a person into understanding the other person. This in turn, is the essence of validation. You validate someone by letting them know that you hear and understand them. Validation does not mean you "agree" with what the other person is saying. Instead, validation sends the message, "From your point of view I can see how you would feel or think that way."

During this technique, it's important to remember that the focus is not on creating solutions. Instead, the object is to understand each other's feelings and needs. You can work on solutions after all "ordering" is completed or at a later time.

Sarah and Larry found themselves talking about the ways they fail to affirm one another in conversation. At first, they blamed the other person for feeling hurt. Sarah would say, "You make me angry when you don't spend time talking with me." Larry would respond, "You frustrate me when you dump all your anger on me and never listen to what I say." Notice how both partners were projecting blame and not taking responsibility for their own feelings and actions. Let's replay this exchange with drive-through listening.

"When we don't spend time together, I feel angry and hurt," Sarah states.

Larry repeats the essence of what he heard Sarah say: "I hear you telling me that you feel angry and hurt because we don't spend time together." Then Sarah has the opportunity to correct any miscommunication. "That's right," she confirms. They would go on like this until Sarah expressed all her needs and feelings regarding this subject to Larry. Stick to one subject at a time.

During Larry's turn as the "customer" he might say, "I enjoy spending time talking with you when we focus on positive things." In turn, Sarah repeats, "I hear you saying that when we focus on the positives, you enjoy talking to me." Larry acknowledges that she heard him "exactly." Sarah does not defend herself, add to, or belittle what Larry said. The "listener" simply repeats back, attempting to truly understand the other person.

Notice that in this dialogue, each person used "I" messages, instead of "You" messages, which tend to project blame. Both shared facts about themselves without judging the other person's feelings or behaviors. They treated one another with honor and respect. This is drive-through listening.

You need to assume full responsibility for drive-through listening. You are stating what you feel and asking for understanding, not agreement or discussion. It's bottom-line communication that directly conveys facts without additional baggage.

Another way to effectively communicate is through the use of *letter writing*. This method can convey your thoughts and feelings while giving you time to think through what you are saying and how you want to say it. You can then read over what you have written and if necessary change what you have said so that you communicate as clearly as possible.

When your husband reads what you have written, he has time to absorb what you have said without having to respond immediately. Letter writing also avoids nonverbal aspects of communication. This can be an asset to both of you, especially if certain nonverbal habits are irritating to one another.

The final communication method is called the "*all you can eat buffet*." This is positive communication in which you serve up all the affirmation you can for sixty seconds. For your husband this may be overwhelming. Spend time praising him and making deposits into instead of withdrawals from his emotional bank account. Withdrawals are negative comments and criticism. Deposits are praise comments and affirming statements, which do not ask for the other person to do anything but to listen.

Tips for When You See Each Other

When you do see one another, it's important for those face-to-face meetings to be constructive. Here are some important questions and tips to consider for those meetings.

How can I foster trust in my husband? Your husband needs to know that you are not just acting but really communicating your genuine feelings. Additionally, you need to be able to trust him. Trust takes time and patience. It cannot be rebuilt overnight. So don't expect the first few meetings to overflow with trust. Both of you will have to see godly change in one another over a long period of time. Trust is built upon transparent, consistent words and actions that embody truth and keep promises.

How can I encourage my husband to accept my influence? One husband said to us about his wife, "I watched her track record. She was obviously more relational than I was. The longer we were together, the better it became. I didn't want to be told what she was going to do. I actually had to see it work. What she said was working so I finally stopped pushing my agenda and started working with her." Let your life bear spiritual fruit. When your husband sees the good fruit of your thoughts and behavior, then he can decide whether or not to accept your influence.

How can I reach the point where his response doesn't determine my actions? You are not reacting to him but being obedient to God's leading in your life and marriage. Winning your husband back does not start with his reactions but your obedient actions to the Spirit's guidance.

Your husband is a subject that needs to be studied. Are you ready to become a student of your husband?

Chapter
Eleven

Become a Student of Your Husband

Even if marriages are made in heaven, man has to be responsible for the maintenance.

—Kroehler News

We love this quote because the message is that although God is the author of our marriage, we still need to proactively take care of our relationship. One of the greatest ways to "maintain" your marital relationship is to learn about your husband's most important relational needs.

Several years ago, Kathy shared how important it is to become a student of your husband.

Growing up in Mississippi meant when you married you stayed married. If my dad was alive today, he would have been married almost thirty-four years. So it's very embarrassing when I tell people that my first marriage lasted for six months. God basically did everything but burn the church down to keep me from marrying this man. But I still followed my own will. Everybody says God just didn't bless it or He just didn't want it to happen. God gets a bad rap in my opinion. Let's not blame God. God did everything in the world to tell me this was not the right guy. But He gives us our own free will. If we fail, it's not His fault.

I remember sitting in a parking lot one day after I'd discovered my first husband was having an affair and crying, "Lord I don't know what to do, but I need a peace whether I should leave him or stay in the marriage." It was almost like an instant peace at that point.

I had to know what a "peace" felt like because it happened again in my second marriage. Another affair. I was devastated. But this time God did not give me a peace to divorce my second husband, Mark. Instead, Christ told me I was not the woman that He wanted me to be. He kind of used these circumstances to teach me a valuable lesson about meeting my husband's needs. I was hurt, but God moved me from being offended and hurt into telling me what He wanted me to do and what He wanted me to be.

As I look back, one issue I was struggling with was that instead of relying on God to meet all my needs, I was beating Mark up because he wasn't meeting them. In reality, our husbands cannot meet all our emotional needs. I tell women all the time that they are asking their husbands to be this perfect, burden-bearing, fixer-upper type person. They aren't. They are just men.

In other words, women can get off on this thing that husbands are supposed to be our protector, our lover, our friend, and they're supposed to fix everything that happens to us. When Mark did not live up to these expectations, I tore him down. Another issue is that my personality tendency is to lead and Mark's is to follow. This caused much tension in our relationship as he attempted to be the head of the family. As a result, I stopped meeting his important relational needs and Mark stopped meeting mine.

This progressed until I learned the hard way that if I'm not meeting those needs there is someone who will. Basically that's what happened. After I discovered that Mark was having an affair, I remember crying, thinking, *What am I going to do?* I went back into my bedroom and read the Bible to see what it said about affairs. I think I was looking for a way out, basically saying, "Well, this is what God says about adultery." But God said it wasn't okay for me to divorce Mark. I truly believe that God was not going to release me from my marriage because there were some things that I needed to fix. Mark was only part of the problem.

It took approximately six months. After the affair, I learned forgiveness and the meaning of unconditional love. I also began to understand and meet Mark's relational needs. And vice versa. For example, when I would put my lipstick on in the morning, it used to irritate him that he couldn't kiss me good-bye. He's an affectionate person. So I began kissing him before putting on my lipstick. That was so simple. But at a deeper level it communicated to Mark that his needs were important.

The Tremendous Value of a Man

Kathy realized that in order to win Mark back, she had to recognize his tremendous value as a man and how to meet his needs. What is the tremendous value of a man? Let's take a look.

We're convinced that most men are willing to take steps to build a loving, lasting relationship. The problem is that the average man doesn't intuitively know how to do this. On the other hand, God seems to equip women from birth with important skills a man tends to lack. In other words, a woman seems to possess a "built-in marriage manual." In part, that is the reason for the special title she bears as a man's "completer" and "helper."

When thinking about remodeling a house, you need the proper tools. You wouldn't use garden tools to do carpentry or use wallpapering implements for painting. Similarly, your husband comes with fewer tools in his emotional tool kit than you do. In the emotional arena, wives come in with an algebra understanding of emotions while husbands function at a level of addition and subtraction.

If you had to build an addition on to your home, it would be very difficult to do your construction with hand tools instead of power tools. Likewise, your husband is working with very rudimentary relational skills compared to those you have in your emotional tool kit.

Lynnda and William came to Gary for counseling. In assessing the emotional outlook each of them had for their marriage, I asked, "Tell me where you see your family."

William replied, "You know, at the end of *The Sound of Music* where they are singing and dancing through the hills? They are all so happy and the sky is blue. That describes our marriage."

Lynnda sat there with a stunned look on her face. I then asked her, "Where do you see your family?"

"It is so cold and dark. We are lost in the woods, and there are big hills and thickets, and we are all cut up from the briers. The sun is going down, and every time we see a clearing, and we think we are out, then there is just another big hill and thicket," Lynnda answered.

Little girls are often raised to assume that boys understand emotions and relationships just as they do. Obviously, William and Lynnda had run into the wall of emotional misunderstanding and miscommunication. William did not understand Lynnda's deep, hurting emotions. He lacked the tools to begin rebuilding a relationship with his wife.

Some women, however, use their natural edge in relationships as ammunition for bashing men and a man's place in the home. Some men have even read some of my earlier books and felt that I (Gary) was jumping on the male-bashing bandwagon. However, we'd like to set the record straight. Although a man generally does not speak as many words or may not be as naturally sensitive as a woman, he is nonetheless capable of being a great lover in the home. Let's take a look at two very important reasons why men have such tremendous value.

1. *Men have a natural ability to make a factual and logical decision to love others.* Believe it or not, God has built into every man the natural ability to be the loving leader his family needs. Saying that God has designed a man to be the lover in a home may sound a bit strange. After all, we spoke of a man's conquering, logical, fact-driven nature, but that very nature is the foundation for our conviction. Why? Because the kind of love that lasts, the kind that can grow and thrive apart from feelings, is the kind that comes from a decision. In other words, love—stripped to its core—is just that, a factual decision that doesn't have to depend on our feelings. A husband has the natural ability to make a decision to love his spouse

and family. Men have an incredible capacity to detach from the hurtful emotions of relational difficulties and make the decision to love and nurture. It doesn't mean that a man will do this—but we want to recognize that they have a natural, built-in capability toward this kind of action.

2. *Men's gender differences can add value to the relationship.* Men and women do have basic gender differences but not the one our culture proposes. Many cultural commentators look at human personality and contend that men have a soul comprised of a mind and will while the female soul is emotions and will. That's not what God reveals.

Both men and women are created whole with body, soul, and spirit. "Now may the God of peace make you holy in every way, and may your whole spirit and soul and body be kept blameless until that day when our Lord Jesus Christ comes again."[1] Paul wrote these words about men and women alike who are created whole in Christ Jesus.

In *For Better or For Best*, I (Gary) examined some of the differences between men and women. For our purposes here, we want to share with you some basic qualities of men that are important for you to understand as you move toward winning your husband back.

You might think of these qualities as using the right materials when building or decorating a house. There are certain materials that you might use in a kitchen or bathroom that would not be needed in a bedroom or a den. To expect a den or a bedroom to have a tub or a shower would be unrealistic. In the same way, to expect men to have certain characteristics would be unrealistic as well. Here's a true/false test. These statements are usually true or false of men. Test yourself and see how well you do.

Put a *T* for True or an *F* for false.

Men are usually . . .

_____ more preoccupied with practicalities than women.

_____ able to keep their identity from becoming entwined with other people and situations.

_____ able to logically and quickly deduce and adapt to change.

_____ higher in metabolic rate than women.

_____ sexually stimulated by sight.

_____ less sensitive to feelings and complex relationships than women.

_____ preoccupied with concrete practicalities, solving problems, and making decisions.

_____ able to detach from surroundings but often identify more with work.

All of these statements are true. Understanding the differences between men and women can help you to reduce the distance in your relationship. It's also important to know that most men were not raised to understand emotional, relational language. They are less responsive to touch. Even as babies, men are picked up less frequently than women. It could be that your husband feels misunderstood and that he fails to understand even the basic realities of your personality and femininity.

The masculine context is to be a problem solver and to make decisions; while the female context is to be a nurturer and to develop intimacy. As you communicate value of your husband's masculine context, you increase your opportunities for drawing closer together.

What Can Keep You from Understanding Your Husband's Value?

Now that we have looked at the tremendous value of a man, let's turn our attention to four specific things you might be doing that can interfere with your ability to recognize and reap the benefits of your husband's natural value. As this happens, it can cause distance within your relationship.

1. *Trying to control and manipulate him.* Lisa Brevere has written a book titled *Out of Control and Loving It.* Isn't that a great title? She came to the realization that she had to surrender control of her life and her desire to control others to the Lord. Are you willing to pray, "I give up control. Lord, he's Yours and I'm Yours"?

Paul urges us in Romans 12:1–2 (NLT),

> And so, dear Christian friends, I plead with you to give your bodies to God. Let them be a living and holy sacrifice—the kind he will accept. When you think of what he has done for you, is this too much to ask? Don't copy the behavior and customs of this world, but let God transform you into a new person by changing the way you think. Then you will know what God wants you to do, and you will know how good and pleasing and perfect his will really is.

The issue in this Scripture is control—will you surrender control of your body and mind to Christ?

Manipulation seeks to force others to do what you want—not what God wants. Manipulation tries to get your needs met at others' expense. True surrender is releasing others to

God's control. You may influence your husband by your godly behavior and words, but when you move from influence into manipulation, you will drive your husband farther away.

God changes people—we don't. And He doesn't need our help in changing them. All God requires of us is to pray and look at our own life.

2. *Emotionally focusing on the children.* Once children enter the family picture, a mother may transfer much of her emotional focus to them. This, too, can cause distance in the relationship. The husband may feel that he has taken second place to the children.

As you allow your children to come between you and your husband, you increase the distance between the two of you. Raising children is stressful. That stress can negatively impact your marriage.

Furthermore, raising teenagers is especially stressful. In fact, research indicates that one of the greatest seasons of unhappiness in marriages is when a couple are raising teenagers. Teenagers can be emotionally draining. If teenagers have come between you and your husband, decide now to focus on winning your husband back instead of communicating to your mate that your children are more important to you than he is.

3. *Following separate dreams.* When your dreams and visions move you both in separate directions, distance grows between you. What dreams do you have in common? What dreams drive you apart? Think about the dreams you both have in the following areas of your lives. Check to indicate that you believe your dreams and your husband's dreams are the same, different, or you're not sure.

Dreams About	Shared	Different	Don't Know
Marriage	_____	_____	_____
Children	_____	_____	_____
Where we live	_____	_____	_____
Finances	_____	_____	_____
Work	_____	_____	_____
Religion	_____	_____	_____
Retirement	_____	_____	_____
Other:_____	_____	_____	_____

Too many different dreams build distance and walls in marriage. And if you don't know your husband's dreams in a particular area of your marriage, then it's time to ask him and listen to his dreams. To paraphrase Proverbs 29:18 (KJV), "Without a vision or dream, a marriage perishes."

4. *Not making your needs known.* No husband is so intuitive that he knows what you need before you ask. Imagine an interior decorator trying to redecorate your house without asking you what you desire. Being married does not qualify either a husband or a wife to be a mind reader. God even instructs us to ask for what we need—and He knows our needs! "Keep on asking, and you will be given what you ask for. Keep on looking, and you will find. Keep on knocking, and the door will be opened. For everyone who asks, receives. Everyone who seeks, finds. And the door is opened to everyone who knocks."[2]

Decide to communicate your genuine and realistic needs. Unfulfilled needs and expectations may have built up in your marriage because they were not communicated. The bricks of unfulfilled needs and expectations become walls of unresolved anger and bitterness that block communication and love.

Reach Out to Meet His Needs

Perhaps some of the distance between the two of you is the result of unmet needs—his and yours. What are the needs of spouses in marriage? While the priority of these needs will differ between the sexes and from person to person, the basic list of needs remains constant for married couples.

Do you ever do something you feel is loving for your mate, but he or she does not respond in a positive manner? One day, a well-meaning husband experienced this same frustration. The man wanted to do something special for his wife so he left work early and bought his wife some flowers, candy, and a card. When he arrived home, he presented the gifts with great pride and exclaimed, "Hi, honey! I love you so much!"

Immediately his wife started crying. "Everything's gone wrong today," she explained, sobbing. "The baby's grouchy, the dishwasher won't work, and now you come home drunk!"

As illustrated by the wife's reaction, sometimes we can do things for our mate to demonstrate our love, but it's not what they need. Many of us understand what we need to feel loved. However, what we need isn't necessarily what our mate requires. For example, my (Greg) wife, Erin, likes me to compliment her appearance. On the other hand, if Erin never mentioned my appearance I wouldn't give it a second thought. Therefore, since I don't need Erin to compliment my appearance to feel loved, I have a tendency not to notice her appearance. This is a common problem couples face: We have a tendency to demonstrate our love in the same manner as we like to receive it. The problem is that our mate may need something totally different from what we may provide. One important factor in marital satisfaction is discovering the specific things that your mate needs to feel loved. In other words, discovering his built-in marriage manual.

One simple way to uncover your husband's marriage manual is by making a list of what he needs to feel loved. We encourage you to set aside several hours of uninterrupted time with him and write down these specific things. As you construct your list, remember not to judge, disagree, or invalidate the things that your husband says. Remember, this is what he needs to feel loved. Also, write down things that are observable. In other words, instead of writing down "I want intimacy," write, "I need you to say you love me at least once a day," "We will make love twice a week," and "I need you to ask me about my day." These behaviorally specific statements can help your husband to translate vague statements into specific behaviors. For example, the people at the Center for Marriage and Family Intimacy in Austin, Texas, have identified a list of the top ten relational needs for intimacy.[3]

Rank these needs according to your personal priorities of what you need in marriage:

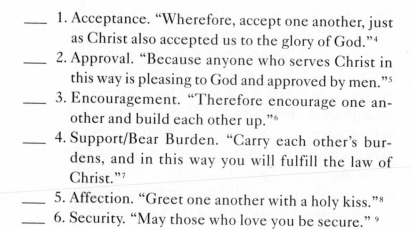

____ 1. Acceptance. "Wherefore, accept one another, just as Christ also accepted us to the glory of God."[4]

____ 2. Approval. "Because anyone who serves Christ in this way is pleasing to God and approved by men."[5]

____ 3. Encouragement. "Therefore encourage one another and build each other up."[6]

____ 4. Support/Bear Burden. "Carry each other's burdens, and in this way you will fulfill the law of Christ."[7]

____ 5. Affection. "Greet one another with a holy kiss."[8]

____ 6. Security. "May those who love you be secure." [9]

___ 7. Respect. "Show proper respect to everyone."[10]

___ 8. Attention. "But that the members [of the body] should have the same care for one another."[11]

___ 9. Comfort. "The God of all comfort, who comforts us in all our troubles, so that we can comfort those in any trouble."[12]

___10. Appreciation. "I praise you."[13]

The needs on this list are general. They are not behaviorally specific. After reading the list you both need to define what each word means to you. Define them so you will be able to know when they occur. For example, the need for appreciation might mean something different to both you and your husband. Explain what it means to you. Then ask yourself how you and your husband would prioritize these needs. Which needs are you willing to reach out and meet in his life? If there are unmeet needs in your life, are you willing to release those to God who is able to meet all your needs?

After you understand what your mate needs to feel loved, then you need to be held accountable to follow through. Your spouse has given you a tremendous gift by listing what he needs to feel loved. You now literally possess your husband's marriage manual. We strongly encourage you not to let this precious information go to waste. One of the best ways to be accountable is by asking a very simple question: "On a scale from zero to ten, with ten being the best, how have I done this week in making you feel loved according to your needs?" As you consistently ask this question, you will be increasingly able to love your husband according to his needs and not your own.

We are convinced that answering this type of question on

a weekly basis could reduce long-standing marital problems. Imagine how low the divorce rate would be if conflicts, hurt feelings, and anger were resolved within a week. The key is remembering that love is a decision and not merely a feeling. Many times we do not feel like loving our mate. You can, however, make the decision to love him by doing the things that strengthen the relationship. We recently read an anonymous poem that emphasizes the importance of making a daily decision to love the people in your life.

> The world we know can be construed for hours
> On a fantasy love filled with moonlight and flowers,
> But real love isn't like that—it has highs and lows,
> And we must keep our direction, however it flows.
>
> I made the decision right from the start
> That I'd always love you with all of my heart;
> So if my pulse stops racing as you enter the room,
> If my sunshiny days turn to gloom,
> If words said in anger cut deep to the core,
> I won't love you less—just perhaps, forgive more.
>
> Emotions are fickle; we can't live by whim,
> Changing affections like chaff in the wind.
> I've made my decision and I'll follow through;
> Love is a decision, I've decided to love you!

You may be making great progress in winning your husband back, or you may be facing the reality that the two of you are moving farther apart. You need to consider this possibility: He may not come back.

Chapter Twelve

What If He Doesn't Come Back?

What therefore God hath joined together, let not man put asunder.

—Matthew 19:6 KJV

The journey of winning your husband back began with a decision that loving God and yourself would be your primary objective throughout this whole process. We are praying that as you and your husband grow closer to Christ, you will begin to reduce the distance between you and become truly one in Christ Jesus. And even if you do not win your husband back, the Bridegroom loves you, and your position in Christ is filled with His purpose and possibilities for your future in Him.

There may be some reasons why your husband isn't coming back now. Consider these possibilities:

- It's not yet God's timing for him to return. God may still be working on him or you, preparing each of you for a future time of reconciliation.

- God uses pain to produce "treasures" in us. This time of distance between the two of you may be a time of God's putting you on the potter's wheel and shaping your life through difficulty and pressure. Learn the lessons God has for you now. If you try to escape the pressure you may miss an important lesson from God.
- You're becoming a stronger, better person in Christ regardless of how your husband responds. His response doesn't determine yours. You can choose to grow spiritually and emotionally regardless of how he behaves toward you.
- Let's discuss one last possibility. You may grow all the violets in the world to share with your husband and you may build the most attractive home, i.e., relationship, possible and he still doesn't come back. You may start becoming all that Christ calls you to be, and still your husband doesn't change. He has some choices to make as well. And it may be possible that your husband is pathologically abusive, angry, or evil. If he doesn't change, you do not want him back.

The final question is simply, "Are you free to lose your husband?" When you are free to lose your husband, you will be free to get him back. He's not yours; he belongs to God. We don't possess anything or anyone. Mates are a gift from God. This is exactly what Patti understood when she wrote her husband the following letter of release:

I've been through some very tough times since you said you wanted to leave nine months ago. My love for you is so profound that I just couldn't face the possibility of life without you. To a person like me who expected to marry only once and to remain committed for life, it was a severe shock to see our relationship unravel. Nevertheless, I have done some intense soul-searching, and I now realize that I have been attempting to hold you against your will. That simply can't be done. As I reflect on our courtship and first years together, I'm reminded that you married me of your own free choice. I did not blackmail you or twist your arm or offer you a bribe. It was a decision you made on your own. Now you say you want your freedom and, obviously, I have to let you go. I'm aware that I can no more force you to stay today than I could have made you marry me. You are free to go. I know now that getting the paperwork started was wrong of me, simply because that is not what I want—a year ago, today, or ever! So, as far as that end goes you should know that I will no longer initiate anything in that direction and that paperwork has been destroyed. If our marriage is to follow that fatal path it rests on your shoulders and is between you and the Lord. We both have to answer to Him in our own way, and my conscience is clear. I will be cooperative if you choose that path and, for a time, I will be receptive to reconciliation.

Move back home or stay out—it's your decision and I finally accept it. I admit that this entire experience has been a very painful lesson for me, but the kids and I are going to make it; we are adjusting very comfortably to our new life. The Lord is with me now, and He'll go with me in the future. You and I (and the kids) had some wonderful times together. I'll always have memories of the good times, and I now look forward to the future, either way. I will continue to pray for you and trust that God will guide you.

The Ultimate "Win"

If your purpose in reading this book has been to set your sights on winning your husband back, you have been short-sighted. Your purpose needs to be to fulfill God's will for your life. If both you and your husband are seeking God, then the desire for Him will close the gap between you. But if your husband doesn't want God's purpose for you and the marriage, then you must be free to let him go. God will deal with him just as He is dealing with you.

If both of you are making a commitment to draw back together in Christ, then your dedication must increase while your talk of separation and divorce decreases and is ultimately extinguished.

Paige desperately wanted to win Alan back. Though they were living apart, an opportunity presented itself to work on their marriage. Alan's mother paid the registration for them to attend one of our "Love Is a Decision" seminars. Paige loved it. Alan just tolerated it. He acted indifferent and unfeeling. While the seminar seemed to reinforce everything Paige felt, Alan was bored and unaffected.

As Paige tried everything she knew to win back her husband's attention and affection in their marriage, Alan's only response was, "You are too controlling." He told Paige that she could always get others to do what she wanted, but he didn't have to give in to her wants or desires.

In spite of her efforts, Alan chose to continue living out of their home. He still lives with a coworker in another suburb. He comes to see their children regularly. He doesn't call their house his house anymore. He calls the place where he lives "home." Whenever he does that, Paige winces and feels a stab deep inside. She recognizes that Alan's commitment to the marriage is continuing to dissolve and wonders what she can do to reverse his lack of commitment to the marriage.

Adding to Paige's pain is the reality that Alan's family will not support her efforts to win him back. One of Paige's sisters-in-law consciously refuses to call Paige her "sister." Alan's youngest sister answers the phone when Paige calls and announces, "Alan, your woman is on the phone." She refuses to refer to Paige as Alan's wife. Paige's in-laws already think of Alan and Paige as being divorced.

What would you do if you were in Paige's situation? Basically, you would have two options: fight or flight. You could fight for the marriage in spite of his response or you could run from the marriage. She stayed committed to winning him back but she didn't make him or the marriage problems the center of her life.

As you seek to win your husband back, some basic commitments need to be made. These commitments are unilateral. That means that you will make a decision to act and then act to win your husband back regardless of how he is presently acting or how he responds to you. The first commitment is to yourself and your relationship with God. The nature of this commitment is: I am committed to growing in body, soul, and spirit regardless of my husband's commitment to himself, me, or the Lord.

You must decide to make a unilateral commitment. You will emerge from this season of your life as a winner whether or not you win your husband back in the marriage. It's important for you to go forward with your life fulfilling God's destiny for you.

Once you have made this primary, unilateral commitment,

a second commitment is necessary. You must decide to work at winning your husband back regardless of how he is responding at the moment. He may or may not show an initial interest in drawing closer to you. Nonetheless, your decision must be to follow through on what we have been exploring—with him or in spite of him. So your next commitment is: I am committed to winning my husband back, with his support or in spite of his lack of interest.

It may take some time before your husband responds. The greater the distance between you, the longer the time may be before he responds to any initiatives on your part.

Summary

Providing that your husband loves the Lord and is open to Christ working in him just as He is working in you, you should begin constructing a new house built according to the basic blueprints we have described within the pages of this book. Let's review the most important steps to take to win back your husband.

1. *Allow Christ to fulfill your life.* We must stop looking at people, places, and things to fill our "cups." Heidi's advice to other women attempting to win back their husbands echoed this same message: "Seek the Lord first and the relationship with your husband second. If you seek Christ and get your own heart right, He will provide the power for unconditional love and strength to reach out when you feel rejected by your husband. In fact, God gave me a wonderful toast the night of my daughter's wedding, 'Love the Lord your God with all your heart, with all your soul and with all your strength.' I did the acrostic for LOTS:

Love the Lord.

Obey the Lord, whatever it costs you.

Thank Him in everything and trust in Him for everything.

Seek Him first and surrender everything to Him.

"The relationship with the Lord, seeking Him, and seeking His Word, and obeying it, must come before 'Love is a Decision.' Then out of our hearts will flow rivers of living water."

2. *Become whole.* Paige learned this valuable lesson when she wrote, "I've seen all kinds of changes in me since my husband left. I think I was a little too needy. I was very independent before we got married. As our marriage progressed, however, I became more dependent on him. What helped me was to remember the specific things I was doing before our marriage that resulted in my being independent. I simply started doing those things again. With God's help, I know that I am becoming whole in body, soul, and spirit."

3. *Pray for your husband.* Amber gave the following encouragement: "Pray every day for your husband. That is the most powerful thing you can do for your husband. It has nothing to do with the makeup you wear and nothing to do with your size. If you are praying for your husband and being the woman God wants you to be, you are going to be the wife your husband needs."

4. *Get support.* Support in the form of mentors, intercessors, friends, and accountability groups is vital during this time. As my (Gary) wife commented, "I now realize how important it was when I was trying to win Gary back to seek support from a group of friends. The group made me realize that I wasn't alone in my pain. Other people were going

through similar things. That was a tremendous source of comfort."

5. *Do what it takes to win your husband back.* Dedication asks, "What is it going to take for us to redevelop, reconnect, and have a good relationship?" The essence of dedication is proactive, not reactive. Stop responding to your husband's words or behaviors and decide to respond based on your dedication and commitment. Establish the level you want the relationship to grow to and then work toward that goal. This produces hope. Dedicated commitment also takes time. Dedication involves counting the cost in terms of time, emotional investment, finances, and hard work in the relationship. Winning your husband back will not be easy. It probably took years to get into your present predicament; you cannot expect microwave success in healing your marriage. Your battle cry should be the same words Winston Churchill uttered, "Never give up. Never, never give up. Never, never, never give up."

6. *Spend time with your husband working on solutions.* Your goal is to shift the focus from problems to solutions. You are no longer going to focus on what hasn't worked, but instead, what has worked in the past, what you both need now, and what might work in the future. In other words, instead of trying to weed out the problems in your relationship, you are going to grow African violets. Moreover, generate solutions that are realistic and give one another hope. Both you and your husband might agree to date one another every Thursday night. During the date share the things you both need to have happen to make a deeper commitment to the relationship.

Dedicate yourself to positive, godly change. First Peter

3:1–2 talks about the power of winning your husband without a word. The power of a changed life—truly honoring him in a godly way without a hidden agenda—will demonstrate to your husband your commitment and dedication to winning him back.

7. *Honor your husband—even when he doesn't earn it.* The old cliché claims that respect must be earned. But honor, esteem, and respect must be given as a gift. Honor involves seeing your husband as a priceless treasure and granting him a highly respected position in your life. Honor also involves serving before one is served and giving before one receives. Honor is forgiving even before the other repents; loving even if one isn't loved in return. We are not urging you to be a doormat. Quite the contrary. Be God's servant. The difference between being a servant and a slave is that God's servant is used by God; slaves are used and abused by others.

8. *Open your husband's "closed spirit."* Anger will wreak havoc within your relationship unless it's resolved. It is like a virus that gets into a computer. All of a sudden, this several-thousand-dollar machine is reduced to a very expensive paperweight. Likewise, open your husband's angry, closed spirit through softness, understanding, the admission of your mistakes, touch, and asking him to forgive you.

9. *Forgive, but do not forget.* Not only can your husband's spirit be closed, but so often your own spirit has been closed as the result of hurt feelings, fear, frustration, affairs, or abuse. When we forgive our mate we move toward being Christlike, we demonstrate love, and it frees our soul. Also, forgiving our mate makes it possible to identify what "treasures" we have gained through our pain and trials. We do not want to forget our pain; instead, learn from it.

10. *Establish healthy boundaries in your life.* If your husband is completely unresponsive, unwilling to make a commitment or become dedicated to working on the relationship, you may have to say, "Pack your bags. You're out of here." This is the essence of tough love. This can motivate many husbands to see the reality and severity of the situation. We have never seen more motivated husbands than when a woman finally says, "That's it." A commitment to tough love demonstrates that you are taking a serious, proactive approach to your marital situation.

11. *Communicate to win back your husband.* Instead of overwhelming your husband by using too many words, fighting without rules, projecting blame, or using harsh words, use a powerful communication method to reconcile with your husband. Drive-through listening helps you follow through with what we are commanded to do in James 1:19, "Let everyone be quick to hear, slow to speak and slow to anger" (NASB).

12. *Reach out to meet your husband's needs*—the needs that you can honestly and realistically meet through God's power and strength. Become a student of your husband's most important relational needs. Again, you will never meet all your husbands needs; only God can do that. But identify one thing, even a small thing, that you are willing to do or say to communicate that you care about him. As Sarah noted, "Sit down and ask your husband what he needs or how you can serve him."

13. *Release your husband to Christ.* Sandi had to make a decision to let her husband go. She grew closer to the Lord and reached a deeper understanding and acceptance of herself as a child of God through this whole process of winning her husband back. Yet her husband isn't back. It has been a difficult

decision but she has let him go. Likewise, you need to be free to lose your husband so you can be free to get him back. Remember that our mate is a gift from God. We must give our mate over to Christ so He can work a miracle.

A Final Word

We have wonderful news for you. Even if your husband doesn't come back, you need to take this journey for yourself to deepen your relationship with God and to be firmly rooted in your identity in Christ. Your beauty and worth come from Christ not your husband. In Christ you win even if you don't win your husband back!

We want to end with the inspiring words of one woman who wrote to us after her husband left. She is in the lifelong process of winning him back.

My name is Stacy and I'd been through a lot even before I was eighteen years old. I gave birth to a son (Kris) at seventeen after I was raped. I've been what my friends call a strong survivor. However, God has been my only strength through it all.

I met my husband, Jim, in 1990. He was so nice and caring but I did not want him for anything but a friend. Later, we began to date. My son really liked and cared about him and my grandparents loved him as well.

In 1993 we were married. Six months after the honeymoon everything began to change. I became bitter toward my husband. He treated me very differently. I then put my effort into a job working with youth. They needed someone who really cared and I needed to care about someone. I wanted more children but suddenly Jim did not. I wanted to talk about my job. He refused to engage in any conversation about my job. Jim stopped being a friend and father to Kris, and I found myself calling Kris "my son" instead of "ours." Of course, the unthinkable happened. I had a brief affair at my job that resulted in another pregnancy. My brother could not wait to tell Jim. Through the stress and turmoil, I experienced a miscarriage.

In 1994 Jim and I separated. Over the next several months we dated but never got back together. I entered into counseling, read every Scripture passage on being a wife, marriage, love, and relationships. I bought books. I spoke and prayed with 700 Club, Focus on the Family, and other organizations committed to relationships. Sadly, I've lost many friends over my decision to remain married.

After more than two years of separation, Jim stopped talking to me all together. It was like my life was over. I cried all the time. But I was left to love him from a distance. I've gone for several years now with only the support of my in-laws. Jim's sisters reject me because of the length of time we've been separated. Jim has left the church and has not talked about reconciliation.

I attend a new church that has provided much support and encouragement. God has done so much in my life. I have a new job working with mentally retarded individuals. I have a deeper desire to be a wife and support my husband. I have made the decision that I want our marriage to work. I take marriage very seriously. My father was married five times and my mother two or three times. I don't want to be divorced. I want to live and die with my husband like my grandparents who were married over sixty years. They died within two months of each other, spending their birthdays together in heaven.

I know that all the relational videos, tapes, and books I read will not bring Jim home. Only God can do this. Someday I hope to write you a letter praising God that Jim has returned. But until that time, I stand strong as the woman God wants me to be. I pray. I fast. I cry. I show Jim love and honor. Most important, I never forget I'm married.

Our prayers and encouragement go with you on your journey toward winning back your husband.

Notes

Chapter 1

1. An "emotional word picture" is a communication device, like a lever, that engages and stimulates a person's emotions and intellect simultaneously. In activating both senses at the same time, the emotional word picture causes us to both hear and experience another's words. Word pictures, no doubt, are a powerful way to take our words right to other people's hearts. But also, word pictures can help others to *instantly* understand you. For further insight into this very powerful communication method see: *The Language of Love* by Dr. Gary Smalley and Dr. John Trent.
2. Matthew 22:37–39 NLT.

Chapter 3

1. Jeremiah 29:11–13 NLT.
2. John 1:12 KJV.
3. Gary Oliver, *Made Perfect in Weakness* (Colorado Springs: Chariot Victor Publishing, 1995), 51.

4. 2 Corinthians 5:17 NLT.

5. 1 Thessalonians 5:23 NLT.

6. Mark 6:56 KJV.

7. 1 Corinthians 6:19 NLT.

8. 3 John 2 KJV.

9. Philippians 4:8 NLT.

10. John 6:63 NLT.

11. Ephesians 5:8–10 NLT.

12. Matthew 6:14–15 NLT.

13. Romans 8:1–2 NLT.

Chapter 4

1. Titus 2:4–5 NLT.

2. Acts 4:36 NLT.

3. James 1:19 NLT.

4. John 8:32 NLT.

5. Matthew 18:19–20 NLT.

Chapter 5

1. Luke 18:7 NASB.

2. Winston Churchill, as quoted in John Bartlett, *Familiar Quototions*, 15th ed. (Boston: Little, Brown, 1980).

3. Romans 5:3–4; 8:28 NLT.

4. Ephesians 3:17–20 NLT.

5. 1 Peter 3:1–2 NLT.

6. Romans 15:7.

Chapter 6

1. Gary Smalley, *Joy That Lasts* (Grand Rapids: Zondervan, 1986), 49.

2. Matthew 22:37–39.

3. John Gottman, *Why Marriages Succeed or Fail* (New York: Simon & Schuster, 1997), 191.
4. Philippians 2:1–8 NLT.
5. Matthew 6:21.

Chapter 7
1. 1 John 2:9–11.

Chapter 8
1. Matthew 6:14–15 NLT.

Chapter 10
1. James 1:19–20 NLT.
2. A. W. Tozer, *Five Vows for Spiritual Power* (Harrisburg, PA: Christian Publications, 1990), 12.

Chapter 11.
1. 1 Thessalonians 5:23 NLT.
2. Matthew 7:7–8 NLT.
3. David Ferguson and Don McMinn, *Top 10 Intimacy Needs* (Intimacy Press, 1994).
4. Romans 15:7 NASB.
5. Romans 14:18.
6. 1 Thessalonians 5:11.
7. Galatians 6:2.
8. Romans 16:16.
9. Psalm 122:6.
10. 1 Peter 2:17.
11. 1 Corinthians 12:25 NASB.
12. 2 Corinthians 1:3–4.
13. 1 Corinthians 11:2.

About the Authors

Gary Smalley is one of the country's best-known authors and speakers on family relationship. He is the author of sixteen best selling, award-winning books along with several popular films and videos. He is a frequent guest on national radio programs such as *Focus on the Family with Dr James Dobson* and has made television appearances on *Oprah*, *The 700 Club*, Cnn's *Larry King* Live, and NBC's *Today* Show. He has also reached hundreds of thousands through his Love is a Decision seminars, as well as through Promise Keepers events.

Dr. Greg Smalley earned his doctorate degree in clinical psychology from Rosemead School of Psychology at Biola University in southern California. He also holds two master's degrees. One is in counseling psychology from Rosemead School of Psychology.

Dr. Smalley is the director of clinical research ad development at Smalley Relationship Center. He is also president of Today's Family, a nonprofit counseling center in Branson, Missouri. He teaches at monthly Love Is a Decision marriage and relationship seminars across the country. Dr. Smalley is an adjunct professor in adolescent psychology at Evangel University in Springfield, Missouri. He has written more than sixty articles on parenting and relationship issues. He and his father, Gary Smalley, are the coauthors of a book for parents of teenagers, *Bound by Honor*. He is also the coauthor of the books *Winning Your Wife Back* and *Winning Your Husband Back*.

Greg, his wife, Erin, and their two daughters, Taylor and Madalyn, live in Ozark, Missouri.